Additional Praise for *Making Rain*

Andrew Sobel cuts through the self-imposed complexity of our business culture with a powerful approach to building client relationships that is refreshingly straightforward, practical, and critically important to everyone.

Tom Taggart, Managing Director, Barclays Global Investors

Making Rain truly captures the essence of what it takes to develop a bond of trust and become a successful client advisor. Full of insight and practical strategies, it's a must read that I have recommended to all of my colleagues.

Robin Bidwell, Chairman, Energy Resources Management

The art of selling and relationship building is truly elevated by Andrew Sobel's powerful science. Readers enlightened by *Making Rain* will eat their competitors for breakfast, lunch, and dinner.

Mike Mulica, Senior Vice President,
Customer Field Operations, Openwave Systems

Andrew Sobel can make rain in the desert. Read this book and bring an umbrella.

Alan Weiss, PhD, author, *The Ultimate Consultant* and
Million Dollar Consulting

Reading *Making Rain* feels like sitting in first class at 30,000 feet, drink in hand, listening to a war-horse senior partner coaching us on how to manage the most critical aspect of any professional's career-creating and sustaining successful client relationships.

Bob Frisch, Managing Partner, Accenture

In this new era of professional sales, the ideas in *Making Rain* are pure gold. Andrew Sobel does a beautiful job of showing how to deliver real value to clients and customers and build long-term loyalty within a framework integrity, trust, and value-added.

Wesley Cantrell, former Chairman and CEO,
Lanier Worldwide

Andrew Sobel's *Making Rain* gives valuable insights into the process of creating client loyalty. Anyone interested in having long-term, profitable relationships with key customers will benefit from this book.

Paul Danos, Dean, Tuck School of Business at Dartmouth

Andrew Sobel is the unequivocal master of building client relationships. He takes us to the next level of consultative selling with this brilliant follow-up to his highly successful *Clients for Life*. In *Making Rain,* Sobel provides insightful, and sometimes humorous, anecdotal examples for how to ally yourself with your clients and sustain lifelong relationships that create multiple business opportunities.

Alan LaFreniere, President and CEO, DCI Marketing, Inc.

Andrew Sobel understands better than anyone how to add value and create true magic in client relationships. *Making Rain* lays out, step by step, the principles and strategies that separate great client advisors from the average professional. It should be a textbook for anyone working in professional services or account management.

Connie Connors, Chief Executive, Connors Communications

Making Rain picks up where *Clients for Life* left off, and it's equally brilliant. Andrew Sobel once again demystifies the path to lifelong client loyalty, providing detailed strategies and tactics that you can adopt immediately. Our organization has with great success grabbed onto his principles, which are as natural and eternal as the laws of thermodynamics.

Doug McKeowan, Senior Vice President, Woodard and Curran

Making Rain is a bible on how to build client loyalty, and it's filled with insight, wisdom, and exciting stories. Developing lifelong loyalty is a lifelong challenge, and rather than pushing a simplistic formula, Andrew Sobel provides us with a variety of powerful and practical strategies to achieve it.

James Kelly, former Chairman, Gemini Consulting, and author, *Transforming the Organization*

Andrew Sobel says that *Making Rain* will help you keep your clients for the long term, and he delivers on every page. It's an extraordinary book, and I found myself underlining and writing in the margin of every page. *Clients for Life* was great, but this is even better. *Making Rain* will be a classic in the field.

Jerold Panas, Executive Partner, Jerold Panas, Linzy & Partners, and author of *Mega Gifts* and *Boardroom Verities*

This subversive book speaks brilliantly to business professionals about developing client relationships, and it sets superlative standards of excellence. It also gives clients themselves the secret codes of consultant candor, boldness, and selflessness with which to design consulting relationships.

John E. Balkcom, President, St. John's College

MAKING RAIN

The Secrets of

Building Lifelong

Client Loyalty

Andrew Sobel

 John Wiley & Sons, Inc.

To Mary Jane, Christopher, Elizabeth, and Emma:
Thanks for the love and laughter.

Cartoons were created by Elizabeth E. Sobel.

Published by John Wiley & Sons, Inc., Hoboken, New Jersey.
Published simultaneously in Canada.

For general information on our other products and services please contact our Customer
Care Department within the United States at (800) 762-2974, outside the United States at
(317) 572-3993, or fax (317) 572-4002.

Wiley also publishes its books in a variety of electronic formats. Some content that appears
in print may not be available in electronic books. For more information about Wiley
products, visit our Web site at www.wiley.com.

Library of Congress Cataloging-in-Publication Data:

Sobel, Andrew, 1955–
   Making rain : the secrets of building lifelong client loyalty / Andrew Sobel.
      p.   cm.
   Includes bibliographical references and indes.
   ISBN 0-471-26459-8 (alk. paper)
      1. Customer loyalty.   2. Business consultants.   I. Title.
   HF5415.525.S63   2002
   658.8'12—dc21

                                                    2002013643

Printed in the United States of America.

10 9 8 7 6 5 4 3 2 1

Acknowledgments

Making Rain is based on six years of research into the ingredients of enduring client loyalty and the strategies that the most successful professionals employ to establish long-term, advisory relationships with their clients. This research has included a large number of interviews with senior corporate executives and individual clients, including over 50 CEOs, about the most valuable professionals they work with. In addition to conducting an extensive investigation into great historical advisors, I have interviewed some of the most prominent living client advisors, and during my workshops also collected the perspectives of thousands of professionals from a variety of fields. I cannot list all of these individuals here, but without their invaluable insight and counsel I could not possibly have written this book.

One of the five "Cs" of relationship capital stands for *companions*—friends and family who nourish your emotional and spiritual side. In the preparation of this book, my family did that and far more. Sitting around one evening with my wife, Mary Jane, and our three children, I proposed my initial idea for a second book on relationship building and asked everyone what they thought. Over the course of the next hour, they made a series of excellent suggestions about its focus and format, and what you see in front of you shares much with the concept that emerged during that family brainstorm—for example, a book with many short chapters and humorous illustrations. Then, my family tolerated with good humor the many weekends and evenings I stole from them to actually write *Making Rain*. Thank you, Mary Jane, Chris, Elizabeth, and Emma.

When I asked my agent, Helen Rees, what an appropriate interval between books should be, her Zen-like response was, "It's time for another book when you have one in you that has to get written." Whether she knew it or not, this is called *empowerment.* Suddenly the next book was up to me, and I was no longer at the mercy of someone else's timetable! A brilliant catalyst, Helen found the perfect editor, Matt Holt, at John Wiley & Sons. Editors are supposed to be gruff and peremptory, but Matt is anything but those things. Supportive, enthusiastic, and creative, he takes time to work with his authors. Pat Wright—technically a freelance editor, but I prefer to call him a *book advisor*—was, as usual, brilliant at sharpening my writing and ideas. Thank you also to Elizabeth Eaton, who created the elegant graphics that you see in these chapters. Finally, thank you to my teenage daughter, Elizabeth Sobel, who drew the cartoons for *Making Rain*. She is a graceful and precocious artist whose work has already been featured in a number of exhibitions and publications. As we put these drawings together, we shared more than a few moments of late-night laughter.

Contents

Introduction:
Learning to
Make Rain
All of the Time

Some years ago, I was subjected to a withering interrogation by the director of procurement for one of the world's largest telecommunications companies. After months of grueling effort, I led a large team that had beaten out five other firms for a high-profile, multimillion-dollar consulting project. Now, sitting in a cramped, stuffy room, the client was cutting and slashing my out-of-pocket *expense* budget.

"I'm going to allocate one long-distance phone call a week per team member," the procurement head snarled.

"But they have families," I protested.

"They can write letters home," he snapped back.

This was looking less and less like the sale of the year—I was going to be a hero at my firm—and more and more like a farm prison for white-collar criminals.

A few months later, an old client of mine—the CEO of a financial services company—called me at home. "Andrew, I know this is short notice," he said, "but I'm getting my top team together next month, and I really need your help. Can you squeeze this in? I want you to lead us through a complete re-think of our strategy." No questions about my fees—he knew he would get great value. No need to explain my methodology—he knew how effective my approach was. And no limitations on my phone calls home.

Isn't that the way it's supposed to be?

It turns out that even the most talented professionals periodically feel the wrath of the procurement director-from-hell who once tormented me. In the course of my consulting work and during the workshops I conduct with a wide variety of professionals, I constantly hear about the pressure to reduce fees and cut prices. I'm frequently asked why some professionals get a steady stream of phone calls from old clients ready to buy while others scramble to find the next scrap of work. How, my audiences wonder, do you break into a client's inner circle of advisors?

In truth, we'd all like to be viewed by clients as an invaluable resource rather than a vendor who's barely on the radar screen. We'd all like to keep our clients for the long term. So if that's your goal, read on—you're in the right place. In this book, you'll learn how to break into your clients' inner circle—their brain trust—and how to reposition yourself as a client advisor rather than an expert for hire. You'll learn how to develop the attributes, attitudes, and strategies that enable you to consistently add value and build trusted personal relationships. The reward—not in every case, but in most cases—will be lifelong client loyalty.

Clients View Many Professionals as *Commodities*

Ten or fifteen years ago, clients lacked basic market and pricing information, and the sales and delivery of most sophisticated products and services required a great deal of client contact. Today, with the click of a mouse, clients can learn practically everything about you and your services, and in some businesses force you to bid in a faceless electronic auction. With another mouse click, they can switch suppliers. Furthermore, the information and expertise once delivered by professionals are being stripped away and made available to clients in a variety of digital media and expert software, just as the *New York Times'* content has been separated from its original paper medium. Less personal contact is required to deliver services to clients, making it harder to differentiate yourself.

To make things worse, clients today have less time available to spend with outside professionals and salespeople. If you want to meet with a client, you are now competing with hours of internal meetings, several hundred daily e-mails, an overflowing voice mailbox, and half-a-dozen projects that have to be finished in the next few weeks. Some clients—often to their detriment—want to make decisions and choices based on an e-mail or brief written analysis, with none of the rich context and insight that a skilled outsider can bring during a face-to-face meeting.

When auditing is automated and requires little client contact, how does a partner with a large accounting firm add value? When 90 percent of Cisco's new orders are placed on its Web site, what's the role of its salespeople? If your distinguishing characteristic is that you're an expert in something, how do you separate yourself out from the inevitable 10 other experts who are ready to take your place, perhaps for a lower fee? The answer is: Add more value, build deeper, more personal relationships with your clients, and go the extra mile for them. *Making Rain* is about how to do these things.

The Value of Making Rain All the Time

In Native American tribes, a rainmaker was someone who could end a drought and make it rain. A rainmaker in our business culture, analogously, snags the big clients and closes the big deals. This magician may come into a stalled sale—a revenue drought, so to speak—and secure the contract while mere mortals stand by and watch.

Would that every corporation, law firm, or political party had one. But such rainmakers are few and far between. Many people feel they are born, not made, and it's not clear that there are identifiable commonalities from one rainmaker to the next, making it difficult to systematically develop more of them. The author of one book about rainmakers, in fact, admits that after studying hundreds of rainmakers, it appears that they come in all shapes and sizes and employ quite different strategies to reach their goals.[1]

Moreover, they tend to be very individualistic, even at times dysfunctional—they can be demanding and disruptive within organizations that increasingly rely on teamwork to succeed. In addition, many rainmakers like to make the sale and then move on, rather than sticking with a client for the long term, a strategy that today often brings accusations of "bait and switch" from clients. Today's sophisticated clients demand value-added from the very first meeting, and it's hard to deliver this value if you're not highly conversant about the client's company and his industry. Under the old in-and-out rainmaker model, this type of knowledge is hard to accumulate.

So hire rainmakers when you can find them . . . but then what? What about your average professionals? What would the impact be of raising *everyone's* ability to add value and create loyalty by, say 30 percent, versus building a business around a few hard-to-manage top guns? The former strategy is both possible and far more likely to succeed.

This book offers a better, more sustainable solution to ending revenue droughts: Making rain week in and week out. You may not get a huge thunderstorm every day, but you will get a steady drizzle that will amply sustain you and create the foundation for great personal and firm success. To illustrate, I offer the following story.

The Tortoise and the Hare

At a consulting firm in Cambridge, Massachusetts, where I began work after graduating from business school, I met William Wallace, a low-key, soft-spoken, and amiable young associate. He seemed to lack, however, the edge that characterized many of the young MBAs at the firm. Although it was easy to be his friend, I sometimes wondered if he had enough drive and ambition to make it in consulting. As the years passed, William did well, but not as well as some. He was always promoted a year after everyone else, and at firm-wide meetings he had a very low profile. Some got on the fast track to partner, but it took William longer to reach that milestone. Almost unseen to the rest of us, however, he was quietly adding value, building trust, and going the extra mile—and in the process cultivating an intensely loyal base of clients.

Five years later, we merged with another consulting firm. In contrast to my own firm, our merger partner had assiduously cultivated a cadre of "rainmakers"—professional business developers who were their front-line shock troops for procuring new clients. I followed, in particular, the career of one of them—a fellow I will call John. He was a hero in the acquiring firm, always bringing home the bacon. When his office was short on sales, they would make sure he was on the road, knocking on doors and getting the orders.

In the meantime, my old friend William began coming into his own. Over the years, he had cultivated several large telecommunications clients, and as the industry deregulated, they needed help— big help. Suddenly, William was bringing in millions of dollars worth of work each year. Then one year, it was tens of millions. The firm made him the head of its telecommunications group, which became the fastest growing part of the business. William soon eclipsed most of us in responsibility and prestige within the firm. He and John, the apparent rainmaker, were running neck-in-neck.

As the consulting business became more competitive, clients demanded deep industry and functional knowledge. John began to falter—he was not very conversant in the actual business issues that his potential clients faced, and he had little industry understanding. His strengths were a strong, outgoing personality, a good understanding of the selling process, and a great golf game. One year he played a desperate gambit: In November, just before bonuses were allocated for the year, he called in to say he had just sold a project worth tens of millions of dollars. We were astonished—was it possible? No one had procured such a large piece of work before. Later we learned that it was a "conceptual sale" that never really materialized!

Meanwhile, William had been so successful—his group, with its thoroughly loyal clients, was practically pulling the whole organization along—that he was named chief operating officer of the entire company. As William's star rose, however, John's grew dimmer.

To help salvage John's career, William asked John to call on some former clients of the telecommunications group. Surely, under the auspices of this large and successful practice, he would regain his former glory as a rainmaker. He sent John to visit an old client, a top executive at a $20 billion company, to see if he could use some of his old "juju" to reinvigorate the relationship. A few days later William got an angry phone call from the executive. "Next time," he said, "don't send the golf pro! This guy knows nothing about my business."

William, the tortoise at the start of our careers, had outrun John, the hare—and most of the rest of us as well! He did it based on *making rain,* regularly, with his clients. Not surprisingly, the same relationship-building skills that enabled William to create long-term client loyalty also served him well in building employee loyalty within his firm.

In today's markets, you win by assiduously building personal relationships with clients, being willing to stick with them over the long term, and adding value every step of the way. Golf and lunch are nice, but they no longer represent real value to clients—they can get these from anyone.

What follows are 28 succinct chapters filled with ideas, tools, techniques, and examples that will help you become an extraordinary advisor who earns long-term loyalty. You'll read about successful modern professionals as well as a number of famous historical figures, such as the Rothschild bankers and Benjamin Franklin, who excelled as advisors and who were masters at building what I call *relationship capital.* You'll hear from a variety of clients as they talk about what they look for in outside professionals. In the last chapter, you will find an assessment framework for both individuals and companies. These assessment tools, which I've developed in conjunction with a leading authority in the field of assessment design, will help you gain an immediate understanding of your own strengths and weaknesses at building long-term client loyalty. The assessments themselves can be found on my Web site, www.andrewsobel.com. They are available at no charge to readers, and you can go there either before or after reading this book.

If you've read my first book on this subject, *Clients for Life: Evolving from an Expert for Hire to an Extraordinary Advisor,* you'll find most of this material brand new but very complementary. *Clients for Life* sets out the seven attributes that enable you to evolve from an expert for hire to a trusted advisor—the "what," so to speak, of building long-term loyalty. *Making Rain* shows you the "how." It illustrates *how* to apply the principles in *Clients for Life* to every aspect of developing and managing client relationships. It also introduces a number of new concepts, such as the Loyalty Equation (Chapter 1); Relationship Capital (Chapter 5); Relationship Growth Strategies (Chapters 16 through 18); and a framework for creating an entire *firm* that is able to systematically build lifelong client loyalty (Chapter 27).

The chapters are grouped into three sections, one for each of the basic stages that we all go through as our roles with clients evolve:

- *Expert for hire:* This is often how a client perceives you when he first gets to know you. The question is at this point is: How do you break out and develop a longer term relationship?
- *Steady supplier:* If you distinguish yourself as an expert, you are often rewarded with steady, repeat business. This is financially attractive, but as a steady supplier you are still a vendor and certainly not part of your clients' inner circle. So how do you evolve into a trusted advisor who is truly an irreplaceable resource for your clients?

- *Extraordinary advisor:* You're now in an enviable position—but how do you develop and sustain an intellectual partnership over the long term? How do you continue to add value year after year?

You will learn, in short, how to break out of the pack as an expert; how to break into your client's inner circle; and how to stay there.

Each of the 28 chapters has a core idea, and each can be read and appreciated on a stand-alone basis. There is, however, a mental model that provides an overarching framework for the various chapters and ties them together. This model can be summarized as follows:

1. Relationships evolve through three distinct phases, and in each phase your role changes. You start as an expert for hire, become a steady supplier, and then, possibly, develop into a broad-based business advisor.
2. Client loyalty is based on the value you add, the trust you build, and the extent to which you go the extra mile for clients. If you want to develop long-term loyalty, you have to do these things consistently—but somewhat differently—during all three of these phases.
3. There are a *variety* of strategies and tactics that enable you to add value, build trust, and go the extra mile. These are described in the individual chapters of *Making Rain,* and they can be grouped into four areas:

   - *Attributes or skills* (e.g., big picture thinking).
   - *Attitudes* (e.g., independence).
   - *Relationship strategies*—the ways in which you apply your skills and attitudes to actual client relationships (e.g., identifying client needs).
   - *Firm strategies*—actions that *organizations* have to take in order to build client loyalty (e.g., idea development through intellectual R&D).

I believe you can change your behavior with clients and alter their perceptions of you. If you do this, you'll see immediate, meaningful results. Just shifting your own self-image from that of an "expert for hire" to a client advisor can create dramatic changes—I have had hundreds of professionals tell me this after they have been exposed to these core concepts.

Remember that small changes in behavior can have a very big impact—enduring loyalty is built on a foundation of many small actions. Any one of the chapters can significantly improve your next client meeting. Taken together, they'll put you well on your way to developing lifelong client loyalty.

PART ONE

BREAKING THROUGH AS AN EXPERT

1

The Loyalty Equation

Three Factors That Determine Your Client's Loyalty

Several years ago, I was in the midst of a long-term project with a CEO who suddenly received an attractive offer to sell his company. After several weeks of negotiations, it appeared the deal would go through. That morning my client pulled me into his office for a talk. I was, in truth, a bit nervous. The company owed me some money for past work, and we had a signed contract for consulting services that extended several months into the future. A change of ownership could throw my arrangements into disarray, delaying or putting into question the payment for my past services and possibly resulting in the abrupt cancellation of the current assignment I was working on.

"Andrew," the CEO began, "I just want you to know that if this deal goes through, I've arranged for you to be paid for the work you've already completed—I don't want that to fall through the cracks, which it might; I'm going to ensure that you are treated fairly." He then added, "I have already spoken to the chairman of our new potential owners about how much you've helped us and suggested he meet you to see if you could be a resource for the combined entity." I breathed a sigh of relief and thought to myself, "Wow, this guy is sticking up for me—he's loyal!" It was a wonderful feeling.

This is, certainly, the kind of loyalty we wish all of our clients demonstrated toward us. We'd like them to keep our legitimate interests in mind, use our services year after year if appropriate, and recommend us heartily to others if they have no further need to engage us.

But what is client loyalty, really? The word "loyal" shares with "legal" a common root: In medieval times, citizens were legally bound to their lord or king through a formal declaration of allegiance. Unfortunately, despite my best efforts, very few of my clients have made legally binding professions of undying loyalty to me!

Today, loyalty has a less strict meaning. Although the term is bandied about rather loosely, it implies faithfulness to somebody or something: We talk about employee loyalty, brand loyalty, customer loyalty, and client loyalty. The conventional wisdom about what inspires loyalty for products or companies, however, isn't all that relevant for professional-client relationships. The reasons why we're loyal to a brand of toothpaste or to an employer are somewhat different from those reasons that compel a client to demonstrate loyalty to a professional who is providing a complex service or sophisticated product. A recent best-selling book on leadership and loyalty, for example, asserts that employees are loyal to a company when the top management is perceived as having integrity and when they feel empowered.[1] *Client* loyalty, however, is based on more than just integrity and empowerment, although certainly both are important ingredients.

I have conducted hundreds of interviews on this subject with both senior corporate executives and individual advisors, and it is clear that there are three main drivers of client loyalty:

1. The value you add.
2. The degree of trust you develop.
3. The extra mile you are willing to go.

Although something as complex and subtle as loyalty cannot be reduced to a science, these three factors can be combined into a client loyalty "equation," as suggested in the following illustration:

Client Loyalty = [**Value-Added**] + [**Trust**] + [**The Extra Mile**]

Let's look at each of these in turn.

The Value You Add

A client's loyalty is tempered by how much value you've added. Generally, adding value means improving your client's condition: helping her solve problems, achieve personal and business objectives, and get critical work done. A client's perception of value-added, however, will vary enormously depending on the client. Robin Bidwell, an experienced client advisor who is the chairman of the global consulting firm Environmental Resources Management (ERM), sums this up very well: "Different clients value quite different things. One client of ours most valued our ideas and intellectual capital and was constantly spending time with our consultants and sitting in on workshops. Another wanted to feel important, and we had to treat him like a V.I.P. Yet another wanted personal coaching and was constantly asking us for feedback and suggestions. You've got to figure this out right at the start if you want to be successful."

Holding a meeting or writing a memo does not, in and of itself, constitute value to clients. Rather, you have provided value when your client perceives that his business or personal condition has been improved.

Although value can be created in many ways, it's useful to think about three broad types of value that build loyalty:

1. *Core value.* The core value you offer will be the result that you have agreed to deliver to the client. A client wants to reduce costs, develop a new strategy, conduct due diligence on an acquisition,

launch a new product, or install a major telecommunications system—and you help him do it. These outcomes are often referred to as "deliverables." The ability to offer or assemble a bundle of integrated services, by the way, can also be an important component of core value for some clients.

2. *Surprise value.* You truly distinguish yourself when you go beyond the agreed-upon value and add "surprise value." This means raising critical issues, providing insights, or making suggestions about how to fix problems that you haven't been asked to address and which the client perhaps wasn't even aware of. You surprise the client by adding value to her business in unexpected ways.

3. *Personal value.* Every client has personal objectives and ambitions, and if in the course of your work with her you are able to further these, you start adding personal value. Personal value could include getting a promotion, leaving a legacy, or just learning from the relationship with you and your firm.

Tom Taggart is managing director for corporate communications at Barclays Global Investors, the world's largest fund management company, and he has hired a variety of professional service firms during his long business career. Alluding to these additional elements of value, he told me, "This value-added could be an introduction to someone who could benefit my goals or perhaps a heads-up about something they learned that could blindside me. They would do this as a value-added for our relationship, without billing me. The real secret is that when professionals do this on a regular basis, they end up making more money from the client anyway, because the relationship is strengthened."

In my research into professional–client relationships, I have found that a common set of attributes and strategies form the foundation for this ability to add value. These include empathy, big-picture thinking, keen judgment, and others, which are discussed in the next chapter.

The Degree of Trust You Develop

The trust a client places in you depends on several important factors. First of all, do you have integrity? Integrity exists when you consistently adhere to a set of sound values or ethics, you are honest, and there is a wholeness or an "integral" quality to your behavior. Integrity also implies reliability and discretion—you follow through on what you say you'll do, and you assiduously keep client confidences. Second, trust is based on a client's perception of your competence to do a particular job. I might trust a babysitter to take care of my children for an evening, for example, but not to take them on a three-day rafting trip. Similarly, a client has to feel that you or your company has the skill to effectively tackle the job at hand. Trust is also based on knowing each other personally—on some degree of intimacy and "face time." We need first-hand experience with an individual to sense whether there are shared values, personal chemistry, and mutual respect.

Dan Scharre, the CEO of telecommunications equipment supplier Larscom, highlighted this element of trust when I asked him about his loyalty to various professionals: "I look at their ethics," he told me. "The professionals I'm loyal to demonstrate the highest standards of ethical behavior. Yes, they have to do a very good job, but if they don't have integrity, it doesn't matter. They have to honestly represent their capabilities to me and follow through on what they say they'll do, every single time."

As individuals, can we be loyal to someone we don't entirely trust? It's possible, but this only occurs in very particular situations, and usually the result is very narrow and transient loyalty. Within a corporation, you might have an alliance with someone, with an agreement to support each other's agendas (a kind of loyalty), but there might be little or no trust in other spheres. In wartime, similarly, one nation might be loyal to another by virtue of a formal treaty, but trust in the true sense of the word might be very limited. An example of this was the United States' alliance with the Soviet Union during World War II, which fell apart as soon as the war was over.

The Extra Mile You Are Willing to Go

When you set aside your own interests and do something *extra* for a client—when a client perceives that you have helped him in some out-of-the-ordinary way and gone the extra mile—the result is often loyalty. A client of mine, for example, went through some financial difficulty and had to implement a major layoff. Over lunch one day he explained that his company was cutting back on all its professional services. Despite the fact that I had an ironclad contract signed with the company that did not allow it to simply cancel the planned work without adequate notice, I turned to the executive and said, "How can I help? Do you need to eliminate or scale back my work with you? Let me know what is best for the company." He was enormously relieved, and we agreed to refocus my work on just a few high-impact issues with a corresponding reduction in budget. The amount cut actually turned out to be pretty small, but my willingness to voluntarily put my head on the chopping block instilled an immense amount of loyalty.

The extra mile can be represented by many different gestures and acts, and sometimes they have little to do with your formal contract with a client. As Steve Pfeiffer, chairman of leading law firm Fulbright & Jaworski says, "If you leave your vacation a day early to help a client meet a critical deadline, it shows you're dedicated and you care, and this builds loyalty. On the other hand, I have counseled several clients' children on the college application process, and helped them find and get into the right school—this has nothing to do with the business aspects of the relationship but everything to do with the human side. It's appreciated and valued."

Going the extra mile builds loyalty because it enhances trust—it shows that you are focused on your client's interests rather than your own agenda. There is something else behind going the extra mile, however, and it's called *reciprocity*. The development of reciprocity as a fundamental practice in our society dates back to primitive cultures. The survival of the larger group was ensured by the willingness of individual members to trade off tasks and favors. In his book, *Influence: The Psychology of Persuasion,* Robert Cialdini cites some extraordinary examples of this reciprocity principle. After the Mexican earthquake in 1985, Ethiopia, a country that could hardly afford to give foreign aid, sent Mexico $5,000 to help with relief efforts. No one could figure out why Ethiopia, a country with millions of its own starving people, had done this. A journalist, sensing a good story, investigated and learned that in 1935 Mexico had sent $5,000 in aid to Ethiopia to help relieve the famine there. Over 40 years later, its government found the right opportunity to return the kindness![2]

With sophisticated clients, reciprocity has to be genuine—both sides will quickly sense contrived giving and back away. For example, presenting clients with lavish gifts, or doing them "favors" that smack of ingratiation will most certainly backfire. In 1510, Niccolò Machiavelli commented on this insincere motive at the very start of *The Prince,* his famous book on princely power and leadership:

> Men who are anxious to win the favour of a Prince nearly always follow the custom of presenting themselves to him with the possessions they value most . . . so we often see princes given horses, weapons, cloth of gold, precious stones, and similar ornaments worthy of their high position. . . . I value as much as my understanding of the deeds of great men, won by me from a long acquaintance with contemporary affairs and a continuous study of the ancient world.[3]

Ideas and insights, Machiavelli tells us, are far more valuable to clients than schmoozing. How little human nature has changed in five hundred years!

When clients feel that you are willing to go beyond the written contract, to go beyond the normal call of duty—and that you have no expectation of getting something back—that's when this "extra mile" principle kicks in and reinforces a client's loyalty to you.

Some clients are less inclined than others to develop long-term relationships. In the early 1990s, General Motor's head of purchasing,

Jose Lopez, achieved significant cost savings for the automaker by extracting large, across-the-board price cuts from all of GM's suppliers. It was a Draconian move that immediately improved GM's faltering bottom line. It also touched off a highly public firestorm of protest that created terrible publicity for GM, and Lopez's strong-arm tactics poisoned many of the company's most important vendor relationships. Ever had a client like Jose Lopez?

Most of us, unfortunately, have had to work with people like this. These clients don't want advisors—they want experts for hire whom they can beat down on price and pit against each other. They don't believe in the value of long-term relationships. Their sense of loyalty—to the extent they have any at all—is fleeting and mercenary. I think these types of clients represent, fortunately, a small minority.

There are several factors that influence the degree to which your client has a relationship orientation. First, the corporate (or family) culture within which your client has to work will strongly influence how you're dealt with. Some organizations have put in tough policies and procedures, for example, to ensure that no outside provider develops "favored nation status." Second, your client's time frame for the relationship will temper his attitude toward you. For whatever reason, a client may view your relationship as a one-off transaction that doesn't merit any investment. Bob Frisch, a managing partner at the leading management consulting firm Accenture, puts it this way: "Sometimes, relationship-building is a bit like game theory. Your client, for example, will act very differently depending on whether or not he thinks there will be another round."

I think it is possible, ultimately, to build a relationship with the vast majority of clients if you can figure out what their needs are and help them solve their problems. Alan Weiss, a well-known client advisor and author, puts it this way: "If you can connect with a client's vital interests and meet his needs, you can build a relationship. It's that simple."

If you can add great value, build both professional and personal trust, and go the extra mile for your clients, your reward will be long-term client loyalty. Loyalty doesn't mean that a client will do business with you when she doesn't need your services, or choose you over others she thinks are more qualified for a particular task. Dan Scharre, the CEO at Larscom, says this about what loyalty *does* mean: "For many years, I've had a good relationship with a very effective sales trainer. Recently, he's spoken to me several times about doing some work for my company, but it's really not the right time for the kind of service he offers. I feel loyalty to this guy, but that doesn't mean I'm going to hire him when I don't have a real need. In the last few months, however, I have *strongly* recommended him to three or four other executives at other companies. Later this year, when the timing is better, I will probably hire him to do some work with us."

What more could you ask for?

2 | Are You an Extraordinary Advisor?

In the early 1990s, Bell Atlantic, the large telecommunications company now called Verizon, made a bid for cable giant TCI. The idea was that Bell Atlantic would be able to use TCI's cable TV network to offer telephone service to customers all over the country. It was a bold move and, at the time, it would have been the largest corporate merger in history. Once Bell Atlantic had a closer look at TCI's technology, however, and understood the difficulty of sending telephone calls over coaxial cable using the technology of the time, CEO Ray Smith began to have second thoughts about the wisdom of the deal. Smith talked to a number of experts about how to proceed, but one trusted advisor—Steve Jobs, the cofounder of Apple Computer—added more value than the rest. Smith describes how the legendary Jobs helped him make a key decision:

> Over several nights, I debated the issues with Steve and he enabled me to make the best decision of my career, which ultimately was not to go through with the merger. Steve is not very

interested in your feelings—he is a straight-shooter who is incisive and very objective. He had strong technical knowledge about the multimedia environment, but also the ability to see the big picture and conceptualize the application of technology that hadn't really been invented yet. He is very direct, but completely discrete and in this situation was completely focused on my agenda. He challenged me and probed, asking great questions. He was, in short, the perfect advisor.

The professionals who develop long-term client loyalty have evolved from experts for hire to client advisors. Experts for hire offer expertise on a transactional basis—their service, frankly, becomes no more than a tradable commodity. Client advisors, in contrast, provide insight and wisdom within the context of a long-term relationship. Like Steve Jobs, they add value in ways that set them apart from ordinary experts. But what are the underlying characteristics of these individuals? What are the qualities that enable them to add so much value?

The seven particular attributes that characterize client advisors are the focus of *Clients for Life: Evolving from an Expert for Hire to an Extraordinary Advisor,* which I coauthored with Jagdish Sheth. If you have read *Clients for Life,* this chapter can serve as a brief review of the personal and professional development that's required to become a client advisor. If you haven't read this earlier book, you will find that this chapter lays out the theoretical basis for the *practical* applications of these seven attributes. They are essential to successfully building and managing client relationships.

It took four years of extensive research into long-term client relationships to define these attributes. I interviewed dozens of CEOs who shared their experiences in working with outside professionals. I spoke with many of the most well-known client advisors from a variety of professions and industries. And I researched the greatest advisors in over 3,000 years of history. These seven attributes can best be described by contrasting the *expert for hire* with the *client advisor.*[1]

1. Selfless Independence

Experts for hire ultimately seek through compromise and deference to please the clients who employ them; advisors exercise selfless independence. Great advisors are devoted to their clients but independent from them—intellectually, emotionally, and even financially (at least in terms of their attitude). To be an influential advisor to your clients, you must look after their interests but also offer independent views, even if they are opposed to beliefs they hold dearly. Selfless independence doesn't mean you are uninvolved with your clients—it is both consistent with the development of long-term, trusted partnerships with clients *and* a necessary ingredient that ensures these long-term relationships are healthy and balanced. Chapter 24 looks specifically at how you can develop what I call the "attitude of independent wealth," a very powerful technique for cultivating your independence.

Sir Thomas More, who was Henry VIII's chief advisor, is a wonderful example of heroic selfless independence. A more contemporary example would be former Attorney General Elliot Richardson, who stood up to President Richard Nixon during the Watergate crisis in 1973.

Selfless independence is a foundational attribute for anyone who works with clients. I believe it also gives you a certain poise, grace, and strength in managing *any* business relationship. As the degree of interdependence between service providers and their clients increases, the checks and balances that independence provides will grow in importance.

2. Empathy

Experts provide answers and tell; advisors ask great questions and listen. The artist Picasso once said, "Computers are useless. They can only give you answers." The great management sage Peter Drucker says he is no longer a consultant but rather an "insultant," a distinction reflecting the difficult, provocative questions he asks his clients. As professionals, we are trained to provide answers, but in many important respects, thought-provoking questions that help clients reframe their issues are more useful. To successfully empathize with a client, you have to tune into his feelings, his thoughts, and the context of his daily life. There are three basic enablers of empathy: Self-awareness and self-control, which allow you to perceive others—independent of your own biases and neuroses—as they really are; humility, including a belief that you can learn from your clients; and keen listening skills.

How do you keep coming up with such great ideas?　　*It's because I am finally starting to listen...*　　*...to myself.*

3. Knowledge Depth and Breadth: Deep Generalists

Experts have depth; advisors are deep generalists who have depth and breadth. "Find a niche or specialty, and make your name there" is still the common wisdom about how to succeed as a professional. The problem is that most people spend their whole careers drilling deeper into their core expertise, rarely investing the time to broaden their experiences and make the knowledge connections necessary for big-picture thinking.

Advisors focus on learning in three different arenas. First, they continually refine and improve their knowledge of their core specialty; second, they become deeply knowledgeable about their clients and the "ecosystem" that surrounds them; and third, they eagerly engage in broad-based "personal learning" that could include studying a foreign language, collecting antique clocks, repairing cars, or playing a musical instrument. All three of these learning arenas relate in unexpected and mysterious ways that ultimately enable you to offer broad perspectives to your clients. If you doubt this and wonder what your hobbies have to do with client relationships, just remember that personal chemistry, shared values and experiences, and just being an interesting person are all key ingredients of healthy relationships, business or otherwise.

At my old consulting firm, the final hurdle for all potential recruits was the "Chicago snowstorm test." You had to ask yourself: "If I were stuck in the Chicago airport with this candidate for eight hours during a blizzard, how would I feel afterwards? Ready to send him packing? Or energized by having learned something and having had a series of enjoyable, provocative conversations over the course of the eight hours?"

Aristotle, who tutored Alexander the Great, was one of the most brilliant deep generalists in history. Contemporary business figures who fit this mold include management sage Peter Drucker and advertising great David Ogilvy.

In this book, in addition to the *Deep Generalist* profile that I've been discussing, I have added a second development path—the *Branded Expert,* which is discussed in Chapter 14.

4. Synthesis, or Big-Picture Thinking

Experts analyze; advisors synthesize. Listen to what clients say about their most valuable and trusted advisors:

- "He gives me a global view."
- "She provides additional perspective and helps me to reconceptualize the problem."
- "He brings big-picture thinking to the discussion."
- "He handles the details, the tactics, but is also able to see the overall strategy."

Clients, in short, treasure value big-picture thinking in their outside advisors, not least because they are often unable to get the big picture from their own internal staff. "The problem," says Bob Galvin, the former chairman of Motorola, "is that where you sit is where you stand. Corporate executives usually look at a problem from the narrow perspective of the particular function they represent."

We are all trained to do good analysis—to break down a problem into pieces and analyze each bit separately. Synthesis, in contrast, is big-picture thinking—finding patterns, identifying key issues, framing ideas in a way that clarifies them, and creating new ideas out of old data. A recent study of the consulting industry by the *Wall Street Journal,* for example, showed that the number one reason why top executives hire a consultant is to gain "new perspectives" on their business. Regardless of your profession or industry, you need these big-picture thinking skills to craft new perspectives for your clients. How do you develop them? The first step is to become a deep generalist. Without a breadth of knowledge, you can't make the connections necessary for good synthesis. Next, you need to develop the techniques and practices that foster the development of big-picture ideas. These include tapping into multiple perspectives, using analogies and simplifying frames, identifying patterns, suspending your judgment, and taking time to reflect.[2]

5. Judgment

Experts make judgments based on the facts; advisors first help their clients avoid bad judgments, and then they base judgments on facts, experience, and their personal value system. Great advisors are always on the lookout for the many well-documented judgment traps that can ensnare their clients—think of the arrogant "groupthink" that bogged Microsoft down during the company's antitrust trial in the late 1990s, or the "prior commitment" syndrome that allowed President Kennedy to launch the ill-conceived and ultimately disastrous Bay of Pigs invasion of Cuba in 1962.

Great advisors, in contrast, avoid groupthink by bringing their own and their client's unique value systems into play when making decisions. The result is often an unusual but highly effective solution.

One of my favorite examples of an historical client advisor with brilliant judgment was John Pierpont Morgan, who was the first relationship banker in the modern sense of the word. With just a few moments of intense concentration, Morgan could make keen judgments involving enormous sums of money, and he was usually right.

6. Conviction

Experts have conviction based on the accuracy of their information; advisors have deep-seated conviction based on personal values and a sense of mission. Clients are deeply moved by genuine, heartfelt conviction. Says Sir Win Bischoff, the chairman of Citigroup Europe and a well-known top management advisor, "If you want to have an impact, you have to have conviction. The authoritative delivery of a judgment is absolutely key." For many famous advisors, in fact, their defining moments have come in making those difficult decisions based on strongly held convictions. Think of Sir Thomas More refusing to endorse Henry VIII's split with the Catholic Church, or General George Marshall, who had the conviction to repeatedly stand up to British Prime Minister Winston Churchill and his own client, Franklin D. Roosevelt, when critical decisions were being made during World War II.

There are some professionals, unfortunately, whose conviction is superficial and pretentious. I have heard many so-called management experts quote from Machiavelli's *The Prince,* for example, yet most of them, I discovered, have never actually read the book and have no interest in the historical context in which it was written—that is, as an instruction book for a leader who Machiavelli hoped would finally unify the war-torn Italian city-states. The day-to-day persuasiveness that you bring to your client relationships should, in contrast, be rooted in your core beliefs and values and your sense of mission as a professional, and the more you are in touch with these, the more you'll be able to resonate with deep, genuine conviction.

7. Integrity That Builds Trust

Experts have professional credibility; advisors build personal trust. When you're credible, clients believe that your data is accurate, your information useful. Trust, which is the glue that holds together every long-term client relationship, goes far deeper. It's a client's belief that you will act in her best interests and personally uphold the highest standards of integrity and competency, both inside and outside the office. When a client trusts you, anything is possible— your recommendations carry more weight, and when you propose an additional sale, your client sees sincerity, not salesmanship.

In the past several years, clients have paid even more attention to the trustworthiness of the professionals they do business with. During the dot-com boom of the late 1990s, outlandish claims were made and many individuals and companies pretended to be something they were not. When the Internet bubble burst in 2001, and huge firms such as Enron and Global Crossing filed for bankruptcy, people felt their trust had been betrayed.

Since developing and articulating these attributes in *Clients for Life,* I've had the opportunity to discuss and validate them with tens of thousands of professionals from a variety of fields, including consulting, law, advertising, accounting, and corporate sales and marketing. I'm often asked: Don't these same attributes serve you well in developing long-term relationships *in general,* not just those with clients? The answer is a resounding Yes! If you are a corporate staff executive, for example, the same principles apply: To add value to your relationship with your boss—to really stand out—you have to become a deep generalist (not just a staff specialist), demonstrate big-picture thinking, show keen judgment, and build a trusted personal relationship.

There are other characteristics and skills, of course—optimism, ambition, and the ability to communicate, to name a few—that are necessary to succeed in business and life in general. The seven discussed here, however, are specifically needed to excel with *clients*. They are the ones that, in your client's eyes, will truly set you apart from your competitors. When you approach your client relationships with the mind-set of a broad-based advisor and infuse them with these seven attributes, you will create the foundations for lifelong loyalty.

3 | Breakthrough Strategies for Experts

The senior management of a Fortune 500 company was convinced that the high turnover of its managers was due to serious weaknesses in its compensation practices. To address this issue, the executive vice president of human resources (HR) convened a summit meeting of internal and external experts. Sitting around the conference table were half a dozen of the company's staff professionals, including the vice president of compensation, as well as a group of consultants from Hewitt Associates, a leading human resources consulting firm. The head of HR waxed on at length about how the company needed to redress major problems in the compensation systems to reverse the exodus of talent. Fifteen minutes into the meeting, Bob Gandossy, the senior consultant from Hewitt and one of its global practice leaders, interrupted. "You don't have a compensation problem," he stated with calm authority and conviction. All eyes turned toward him. "Systemwide attrition is rarely caused by lapses in compensation. That's not why you're losing people. People leave managers—they don't leave companies. We need to look at your fundamental management practices to find the answer."

As the meeting descended into a cacophony of different conversations, the executive vice president of HR had already made up her mind: Gandossy was going to be her consultant for the job. Instead of selling a small project to review compensation, Hewitt developed a long-term, multimillion-dollar relationship with this client that focused on a broad set of changes in supervisory practices, delegation, and career management, with a consequent decrease in turnover. By effectively *reframing* the client's issue, Gandossy successfully broke out of the pack and distinguished himself as someone able to add more value than the typical HR consultant.

When you first start working with a client, you are typically positioned as an expert: Clients hire you because they perceive you have expertise, experience, and a set of products or services that can help them solve a pressing business issue or enable critical work to get done. Ironically, while clients ultimately treasure the valuable role that a trusted advisor can fulfill, they don't typically go out looking for an advisor—usually, they want an expert. The trick, then, is to demonstrate great subject matter knowledge *and* the skills and behaviors of an advisor.

In this chapter, I discuss nine strategies you can use, in the early stages of a relationship, to differentiate yourself in your clients' eyes and move closer to their inner circle.

1. Do It Faster

Responsiveness is valued by almost everyone, and if you meet your client's deadlines and demands, this alone will put you one notch above your competition. If a client asks for a document on Friday, get it to her on Thursday. If a client leaves you a voice message, get back to her within an hour or two. More than once I have answered inquiries from prospective clients within minutes of their leaving a message or e-mailing me, and every time I am greeted with sincere gratitude and a bit of incredulity: "Thanks so much for getting back to me this quickly!"

2. Do It Better

Some things never change: There is simply no substitute for quality, completeness, thoughtfulness, creativity, and accuracy that exceeds what your client is used to or has seen from your competitors. If you want to become a steady supplier—to gain repeat business right from the start—just demonstrate that you are *better* than the next expert!

3. Be Different or Clever, Not Corny

After sitting through nearly a dozen pitches from bankers wanting to take his company public, Intraware CEO Peter Jackson told investment banker Frank Quattrone that he would "feel like a mule" traveling all over the country to attract investors. The next morning, Quattrone had one of his junior bankers stand in Intraware's lobby with a live mule and a sign imploring Jackson to choose Quattrone's firm, Credit Suisse First Boston, to lead the initial public offering. Credit Suisse did indeed get the business, and Jackson later acknowledged that the mule "may have made the difference."

Sometimes, efforts to stand out can flop disastrously—just ask any executive recruiter about the multicolored, scented resumes he receives that go right into the circular file—but a clever, original approach can sometimes tip things over the edge to your favor.

4. Be Better Prepared

In John Grisham's novel *The Firm,* Mitch McDeere, a brilliant third-year law student, goes to an interview with a secretive but intriguing law firm. Halfway through the conversation, Lamar Quin, one of the lawyers interviewing him, criticizes Mitch's modest undergraduate degree, saying, "I don't imagine Western Kentucky is much of an academic school." What happens next astonishes the staid partner:

"Sort of like Kansas State," Mitch replied. They froze, all of them froze, and for a few seconds stared incredulously at each other. This guy McDeere knew Lamar Quin went to Kansas State. He had never met Lamar Quin and had no idea who would appear on behalf of the firm and conduct the interview. Yet, he knew. He had read the biographical sketches of all of the forty-one lawyers in the firm, and in a split second he had recalled that Lamar Quin, just one of forty-one, had gone to Kansas State. Damn, they were impressed.[1]

My father, a man of meticulous organization, used to tell me, "There is no substitute for genuine *lack* of preparation." It's an ironic phrase that alludes to the disasters that lack of preparation can cause. Some professionals I know are so quick on their feet that they can go into client meetings with only a modicum of preparation, but they are the exception, not the rule—there is nothing worse, in fact, than scrambling to remember the basic facts about your client's company and issues.

Surprisingly, I've had quite a few clients tell me stories about professionals who show up for an initial meeting with little or no knowledge about the clients' company or industry. The threshold to appear better prepared than the next person may be lower than you think!

5. See the Problem Anew

In the opening example of this chapter, consultant Bob Gandossy reframed the Fortune 500 company's issue from a compensation problem to a systemic issue involving a variety of interrelated management practices. This ability to reframe the client's issue—to zero in on what the problem *really* is—is one of the hallmarks of great client advisors. The willingness to act on it is a mark of self-assurance. Both are enormously valuable to clients. It is almost always productive to challenge your client's definition of the problem—in the worst case, you'll simply have to back off; at best, you'll distinguish yourself.

6. Provide Unique Information

In a world where clients have instant access to almost unlimited data, there is still great power in providing unique information and insights. Connie Connors, who heads Connors Communications, a well-known public relations firm, told me about a new client who was participating in a large request for proposal (RFP) to the board of education in New York City: "As it turned out, through several of my contacts I was quite familiar with this RFP, and I was able to provide information to my client on who the other competitors were and advise her generally on how to maximize her bid. This was a value-add on that really surprised and delighted her." Unique information can come from many sources: knowledge of competitors, proprietary market research that you've conducted, customer interviews, and key relationships that you maintain with thought leaders in your client's industry. In Chapter 23, we'll see how the Rothschild banking family used proprietary information to create an overwhelming competitive advantage for itself.

Your information and insights have to be relevant. I knew one "guru" who kept telling his clients interesting and even brilliant things that were completely unactionable and impractical. Finally, one exasperated client blurted out to him, "I just don't know what I'm supposed to do with that piece of information!"

7. Establish an Emotional Connection

Listen again to Connors, as she talks about establishing the personal relationship that brings you into a client's inner circle: "To take your client relationships to the next level, you've got to experience an emotional breakthrough. This has to be based on face-to-face, honest, open communication that creates some kind of emotional bonding. Sometimes this happens when you have a disagreement or an argument. I had a client, for example, who put out a press release at five in the afternoon. That night, I picked it up on a search and, after reviewing it, thought it was poorly done.

I called my client at eight in the evening, and told him what I thought. He was furious—'I've had one hell of a day,' he told me, 'and the last thing I need is my agency telling me I've done a lousy job!' On reflection, the release was not as bad as I first believed, and in fact he was at least partially right—I probably should have waited for a better time to discuss it with him. I apologized profusely for being insensitive. The next day, *he* called me to apologize in turn for having flown off the handle about a minor issue. Our relationship really started to grow from that point onwards."

8. Be Readily Accessible

How often do you call someone and get voice mail instead of a live voice—and then wonder how long it will take to have your message listened to by a living, breathing human? Have you ever sent an e-mail with an attachment, and since you don't get a reply, wonder if the recipient ever received it? Have you ever disputed an invoice, only to have the process linger on for months and require multiple phone calls to resolve? Ease of use, surprisingly, can differentiate one provider from another. It includes things like:

- The ability to get in touch easily.
- Speed of response and the *personal* nature of the response.
- Rapid resolution of accounting and billing questions.
- A feeling, on the part of the client, that he is recognized when he calls your office. (I've had executives tell me that they spend over a million dollars a year with a company, and when they call, no one recognizes them!)
- Demonstrated knowledge of the account on the part of support staff and junior professionals. It's immensely reassuring to a client when he calls about an important document, and someone in your office knows exactly what the client is talking about.

9. Listen and Learn Fast

Last year I sat in on an interview that my son had with the head of admissions at a college to which he was applying. I'm usually very observant, but that day I noticed nothing special about the woman's jewelry or clothing. At the end of the one-hour interview, my son said to the admissions director, "I notice you're wearing an Outward Bound pin. Are you a graduate?" Indeed, she had a tiny pin on her dress that had completely escaped my notice. "Oh, yes," she beamed. "This past summer I finally took one of their adult courses—it was something I had wanted to do for years." The two of them then spent 10 minutes excitedly exchanging war stories about their respective Outward Bound experiences. (This story also illustrates the previous point: You break through when you make an emotional connection with someone.) Listening and learning can be as simple as noticing the little details, or something as profound as investing the time to do a complete analysis of your client's competitive position in the marketplace. The more you observe and learn about your client, the more likely it is that you will stand out from the crowd of experts who are also trying to get in the door—or in my son's case, from the crowd of other high school seniors! (He did, by the way, get accepted at this college, which was his first choice.)

If you're meeting with a new, potential client, or you're in the early stages of the relationship, think carefully about how you're going to break through as an expert. Will you focus on being better, faster, or different—or all three? Can you find opportunities to establish an emotional connection and bond with your client? Do you have some unique and useful information that you can supply? Would enhanced accessibility be valued by your client? Can you be bold and reframe the client's issue?

Clients can make rapid judgments about the professionals they work with, and you may not have the luxury of time to prove yourself. By adopting the right mix of these breakthrough strategies, you'll greatly improve the odds of getting hired in the first place and, later on, of breaking into your client's inner circle.

4 | Building Trust in the First Ten Minutes

Michael, a client of mine, used to be permanently tethered to a PC-powered 50-page PowerPoint presentation. He dragged his laptop around like a ball-and-chain as he visited prospective clients at Fortune 500 companies all over the United States. For every ten clients who viewed his presentation, two would ask him for a proposal, which he would dutifully e-mail to them a few days later. For every ten proposals he wrote, he would win one. The arithmetic was miserable: 50 presentations to get one job. Something wasn't right, and my affable, intelligent friend knew it.

Michael presented himself as a vendor—an expert for hire—and he simply wasn't building trust and credibility in his client meetings. Today, Michael's batting average has gone from 1 in 50 to nearly 10 in 50. He enjoys meeting with prospective clients, and he enthusiastically networks within the organizations of his existing clients. At the end of this chapter, I'll share with you a remarkable letter he recently wrote to me. But first, let's look at four factors—the same ones that Michael learned to use—that affect the degree of trust clients will place in you when they first meet you. We first mentioned these factors in Chapter 1 when we looked at the ingredients of client loyalty. Now we'll examine them in the context of a first client meeting.

Integrity

Discernment between right and wrong, a coherent value system, consistency, and reliability are the foundations of integrity. In the first couple of meetings with someone, these intangibles are communicated through the little things: Are you consistent in how you describe yourself? Do you give credit where it's due? Is there openness to your communication and body language? Do you answer tough questions honestly and straightforwardly, especially about your experience and capabilities? Are you focused on your client and his needs, or are you absorbed in yourself and your own agenda? Your client will immediately pick up any obfuscation or inconsistency.

Michael already had strong integrity, but it didn't come across to his potential clients. His focus was on his own presentation and on trying to demonstrate his personal expertise—not on his client's issues. This misalignment prevented any real rapport from developing.

Competence

A client's trust in you rests in part on his or her perception of your competence to perform a certain type of work. Many professionals, unfortunately, try to establish credibility by *saying* how competent they are. "We have 58 offices in 20 countries . . . we have 10,000 associates . . . we've worked for 300 of the Fortune 500 . . . and so on. Would-be advisors make such claims, invariably with the help of high-tech projection systems and colorful graphics."

This was what Michael used to do—he felt all the statistics in his PowerPoint slides would win over skeptical clients. On the contrary, clients are bored to tears by such assertions and no more assured of a professional's competence.

Recently, an incident involving a major software company underscored why clients are so skeptical of such claims. The company's CEO announced at a press conference that "many leading corporations, including General Electric, are running their entire organizations on our software." When one journalist actually checked, the statement turned out to be a gross exaggeration—General Electric told him that one small factory in Latin America was testing the software in question, a far cry from using it run the whole company's operations! The CEO was subsequently skewered in the press.

A far better way to establish competence is by asking thoughtful questions that implicitly show your expertise and by describing examples of past client work that you've done. Good questions demonstrate an understanding of the issues: "Can you talk about your relative emphasis on domestic versus international expansion?" or "What is the balance between organic growth and acquisitions in your new strategic plan?" are far more useful questions than "What are your sales?"

Client examples are much more interesting and build credibility faster than bland descriptions of what you do. Rather than pulling out a deck of PowerPoint slides, you might say, "Perhaps the best way to describe what I do is to talk about a couple of recent client assignments."

These examples should have three parts to them: the problem the client faced and the pain he or she was feeling; what you did to solve the problem; and the results that were achieved. Two hundred words, at most, are plenty—you want to be able to describe several of these examples over a five-minute period. You'll be amazed at how a good, brief example can establish credibility, draw out a client, and get her to talk about her own issues.

Stand-up presentations have their place, but they tend to kill open, informal dialogue and ultimately put you in the position of a "vendor" who is "pitching" something rather than an equal who sits on the same side of the table to discuss important business issues. If and when you do make a slide presentation to a client, it should be all about the client and his issues, not about you and your firm.

If you already have a relationship with the client, case histories or examples are also useful to reposition yourself and your capabilities. I recently learned that a client of mine, the CEO of a financial services company, needed advice on salesforce effectiveness and institutional relationship management. But he told one of his lieutenants that I probably couldn't help since I focused on "improving relationships with high net-worth individuals." How he got this rather narrow idea I don't know, but I quickly corrected the misperception by describing to him four different clients I have worked with on similar issues. He quickly reached out to me for help. In retrospect, a preemptive discussion on my part to broaden his understanding of my capabilities would have been smart.

Intimacy and Rapport

Clients do business with people they like, and one of the main drivers of "likability" is familiarity (see Chapter 7 for an in-depth discussion of this subject). The more face-to-face meetings you have with a client, the higher the odds that you'll win the proposal. If it's a competitive situation, more meetings will dramatically increase your odds of winning, assuming even a modicum of personal chemistry. More face-time means more chances to understand a person's integrity—her values, her consistency, her reliability—and more opportunity to see if there are shared interests and beliefs. My client Michael, unfortunately, had not yet created the dialogue that would allow this intimacy to develop.

Today, harried clients often want "mail-order" proposals—"Just shoot us something by e-mail," they'll tell you. You might as well mail it to Santa Claus at the North Pole and then light a candle. Your success rate on such opportunities will rarely make the required investment worth your while. Today, when clients ask Michael to e-mail them a proposal, he offers a simple alternative that is almost always accepted: "Let's meet again next week, and I'll walk through an outline of how I would approach this assignment."

Risk

I know a very successful executive coach who refuses to be paid until his clients have been able to verify real personal change. His fees are delayed—sometimes by as much as a year—but his guarantee of *actual results* has resulted in a waiting list of clients and fees that are at the top of the market. I'm not recommending this approach for everyone, but it clearly illustrates the power of reducing risk for clients.

The trust a client places in you will vary depending on his perceived *risk* of trusting you. If there is a feeling that you will stand by your commitment to excellent work—that there is an implicit if not explicit guarantee—then risk is reduced. Patricia Fripp, a well-known professional speaker, often punctuates her speeches on customer service by telling her audiences, "I *guarantee* that these techniques will improve your ability to retain customers." Does she hand out warranty cards? No, her intense personal conviction and energy are enough to back her claims. The result? Her audiences are far more willing to go away and try something new and unfamiliar—itself a guarantee that *some* positive change will occur.

"Every one of our 50,000 associates is ready to be your trusted partner."

What I have described may be simple, but it works. When clients meet you for the first time, they think of you as an expert in solving a problem they have. The approach I've set out allows you to demonstrate your *expertise* while behaving like an *advisor*—a powerful combination. It also sets the stage for broadening the relationship further down the road.

Shortly after he began to work on implementing these principles, Michael sent me a letter. He was in a state of delighted shock at how just a few small changes in his approach were dramatically improving his ability to build trust and establish credibility with clients:

Dear Andrew,

While I was driving to my meeting with this prospective client (a Fortune 500 corporation), I was thinking about your suggestion to use short client cases and thoughtful questioning to help clients understand what we do and build credibility—and your advice to stay away from the PowerPoint presentation and instead focus on the dialogue with the client.

When I joined the meeting on Friday morning, I was surprised to find a room of 11 people instead of just two. I was put at the end of the table and asked to talk about our global capabilities. My first reaction was, Oh no! But then I thought, here is my chance to take a risk and get outside my comfort zone. So, I set aside my laptop with the PowerPoint slides and just spoke about two recent client assignments with major companies. I could not believe how engaged the audience was, what excellent questions they asked, and how much credibility I built. I didn't realize the sense of freedom one has not using a presentation. I still covered all the information I wanted without using the document. The client seemed to trust me after that session, and we are now discussing a major proposal.

Take care and thanks again for all your help and advice.

Michael

It may seem like a very small step that my client took, but I can tell you that his enthusiasm for going out and meeting with new clients and rekindling relationships with old ones has *soared* because of the experience he describes—and so has his income.

5

More Important Than Your 401(k)

Building Your Relationship Capital

While interviewing CEOs and senior corporate executives for this book, I noticed a distinct shift in emphasis and tone compared to similar discussions I held in the late 1990s. Then it was clear that clients gravitated toward professionals they knew and trusted, but now this tendency is even more pronounced. Clients are asking, more than ever, "Whom can I trust?"

What's changed? Quite a bit, in fact. First, the dot-com collapse of the late 1990s left many clients feeling burned by the outlandish, hollow claims that became routine during this business bubble. Second, major corporations such as Enron, Cendant, and Waste Management—as well as a handful of leading financial institutions and professional service firms—have, in recent years, been involved in scandals characterized by lying, financial obfuscation, and putting client and customer interests last. Finally, the September 11, 2001, terrorist attacks gave all of us a renewed sense of the importance of our closest, most trusted relationships.

We have entered into what I call the networked age or the age of *relationship capital,* and the implications for business professionals are profound. It means that your success will depend more than ever on your ability to develop trusted relationships with clients and on the general richness of your personal network. Listen, for example, to Fred Lawrence, a former top Sprint executive and current partner with a leading venture capital firm: "When someone comes in with a new idea and wants funding, chances are that five other people also have the same idea. The real question is, does this person have the network of relationships that will allow him to hire a management team, acquire his initial customers, and develop business partners who can provide leverage?"

Let's put this observation into some historical perspective. In the agrarian age, wealth and position were inherited, and the chief asset was land. Wealth, therefore, was concentrated in royalty and nobility. During the industrial age, financial capital became preeminent, and the greatest wealth was created by bankers and the industrialists who deployed that capital into transportation and factories—people such as J. P. Morgan, Henry Ford, and John D. Rockefeller. For the last 20 years, intellectual capital has reigned; ideas, rather than land or money, have been the currency of the information age. Not surprisingly, our most wealthy and famous business figures today are people like Microsoft's Bill Gates and Oracle's Larry Ellison.

We are quickly transitioning, however, into yet a fourth era: the networked age, where individual and corporate successes are increasingly determined by relationship capital. Our technology emphasis echoes this shift: Whereas the focus from 1980 to 2000 was making more complex software and faster chips (to manage information), the focus now is clearly on the number of *interconnected nodes* on a network and *connection speed* (bandwidth), required both to foster and manage relationships.

The ability to leverage a network of relationships, in short, is becoming more important than just ideas or information. Several forces underscore the importance of building relationship capital:

- Mergers and acquisitions have grown, leading to great transience in the corporate world.
- Job switching has increased, from four to five times in a career to seven to eight times.
- All business professionals—whether corporate employees or independent professionals—are in a sense free agents.
- Many forces, such as the Internet, expert software, and digital technology, are turning most products and services into commodities. It's the value-added relationship *around* these products and services that makes them especially valuable to clients.

Haven't relationships always been important? Yes, but there have always been significant barriers to building them—and these barriers have finally fallen, as illustrated here:

Our Ability to Build Relationships Has Grown

THEN ➡	*Now*
Class Rigidity	Democratization
Wealthy Few	Broad Affluence
Geographic Isolation	Cheap Travel & Communications
Sexism and Racism	Greater Equality
Cultural Insularity	Global Culture

Compared to what was possible fifty or one hundred years ago, today's business professionals have unparalleled opportunities—if they are tenacious and skilled—to build relationships with a wide variety of individuals.

What constitutes your relationship capital? There are five types of individuals with whom you need to build relationships. One of them, of course, is clients, but what I have observed is that the most successful client advisors also have an abundance of the other four types. In fact, these other relationships are essential to their ability to develop and keep clients. Let's look at each of these briefly:

- *Clients and customers.* These are the people and organizations we do business with. They are the lifeblood of service professionals and executives who work in sales and marketing. *Making Rain* is especially focused on developing this aspect of your relationship capital.
- *Counselors.* Counselors advise and mentor us during our careers, providing support, encouragement, and guidance. A number of new studies have demonstrated the importance of mentors in our professional career, and this is especially true for women and minorities who have traditionally had fewer role models to guide them.
- *Catalysts.* A rare breed, these individuals can introduce us to others and make deals happen. Catalysts have a particular personality and way of operating—they can be impatient and even difficult—but having a relationship with the right catalyst can transform a business opportunity overnight. Catalysts are often bankers, venture capitalists, and agents—but they can come in many guises. My literary agent, for example, is a classic catalyst. I once called her to tell her about a particular concern that I had (a very minor one, I might add), and she responded, "You know, Andrew, I'm just not very good at handholding with authors." Maybe she was not good at handholding, but she is a superstar when it comes to making a literary deal happen!
- *Collaborators.* These can be business partners but also individuals we might hire into our organization. An accountant might be an important collaborator for a financial advisor, for example, just as family practitioners are collaborators for the medical specialists they recommend to their patients. My network of collaborators includes a variety of other professionals with whom I exchange information, share referrals, and sometimes work on an ad hoc basis.

- *Companions*. These represent the final category of relationship capital. Companions are family and friends—a class often ignored by today's workaholic professionals—who nurture our emotional and spiritual side. Companions help us to be effective with our clients in many direct and indirect ways. Above all, they provide needed balance to our lives, giving us the emotional stability and strength to deal with difficult moments at work. They also often serve as *counselors* to us, acting as sounding boards and providing calm advice when we are puzzled or uncertain about a particular situation. Usually, our family and friends are able to put our interests first when listening and giving advice. Noting this point, Eileen Friars, a former top Bank of America executive, said to me, "Why is it that many men turn to their spouses when they need a trusted advisor? Because each one knows she has only his interests at heart."

There are two important points to remember about these different types of relationships. First, there can be overlap—it is quite possible for someone to be both a counselor and a catalyst for you, or to be a client and a collaborator. For example, I worked with one client as a strategy consultant (a counselor) but also collaborated with him by jointly authoring an article. Similarly, a few of my clients have become personal friends. That said, there are important distinctions between these roles, and each offers a different kind of added value.

Second, in serving your clients, you need to be clear about which role you are playing and what your client really wants from you. Chuck Lillis, the former CEO of cable giant MediaOne (now part of AT&T Comcast), told me an interesting story in this regard about his advisors: "We were involved in a major transaction with another Fortune 500 company and my advisors included legal, public relations, and consulting professionals. In all three cases, there were specific individuals who added value way beyond the contractual work. It turned out that our attorney personally knew two of the board members of the other company; the public relations guy knew their investment bankers, and our consultant owned a house on Martha's Vineyard right next door to the CEO. A mid-priced consultant would have come up with some complex strategy—this person ended up inviting the CEO over to his house, and it helped to cut through a lot of issues." In this particular case, these advisors' ability to act not only as counselors but also as *catalysts,* made them truly stand out.

When present in balance and abundance, our relationship capital—customers, counselors, catalysts, collaborators, and companions—form the foundation for our professional success and our personal satisfaction. But how do we build these relationships? It's useful to think about four phases of relationship building:

1. *Affiliating.* This is the process of meeting people and getting them interested in knowing you better or doing business with you. Chapter 7 explores the roots of "likability" and how we can increase the odds that others will want to move ahead and develop a relationship with us. Many would call this step "networking," but I prefer to use *affiliating* because its root meaning better reflects the concept of finding common interests.

2. *Adding Value.* For a relationship to work, you have to add value—this is what eventually shifts someone from being a mere acquaintance to becoming a loyal fan. Virtually all of the chapters in this book focus on different ways of adding value. Part of the secret of creating loyalty is properly understanding what constitutes "value" for each of your clients. My earlier book, *Clients for Life,* looks specifically, from a developmental point of view, at the qualities you need to develop to do this. (Chapter 2 also summarizes these attributes.)

3. *Sustaining.* One of the biggest problems for professionals is sustaining relationships over time, especially when they provide a service or a product on a periodical basis (for instance, consulting). Sometimes, years will go by before a client needs their particular service again—so what do they do in the interim to stay in touch? Successful client advisors use a variety of techniques to

maintain contact and periodically appear on their clients' "radar screen."

4. *Multiplying.* This is the fourth and most neglected stage of relationship development. Just as our savings and retirement plans grow in value to us, so should our most established relationships. There are many ways of multiplying your influence through established clients—the two most common ones are through the printed word and referrals. These and others are discussed in Chapter 20, "Sustaining and Multiplying."

These various elements are summarized in the following figure:

Growing Your Relationship Capital

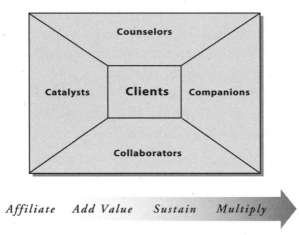

The great client advisors I've studied typically have an abundance of relationship capital. Their ability to develop rich, enduring client relationships is underpinned by supporting relationships that include catalysts, collaborators, counselors or mentors, and companions. Whereas experts for hire focus on networking and adding value narrowly (e.g., fulfilling the specific deliverables of the contract), advisors are adept at all four stages of relationship building. They add value that goes well beyond stated client needs. They invest to sustain their relationships over time, and their best clients help them leverage and spread their ideas and influence.

It is useful to think about your professional career as a drama with both leading characters—your clients—and supporting ones such as catalysts and collaborators. Remember that affiliating with people—what we traditionally call networking—is only the first act of a four-act play.

How do you know how well you're doing at building relationship capital? Ultimately, success should translate into professional prosperity and personal satisfaction with your career. But these are hard to quantify. Furthermore, you could have great relationships but not make them work for you—you could be weak, for example, at marketing yourself and representing your capabilities. The best approach, I think, is to periodically ask yourself the following key questions:

- Do I consistently follow up with the people I establish relationships with, adding value and sustaining them—where appropriate—over time?
- Do I consciously seek to build relationships with a variety of professionals and organizations that can play the roles of collaborator and catalyst?
- Do people in a position to refer clients to me actually do so? If not, what action can I take to develop more referrals?
- Who can help me build my client base, and what can I offer that contact?
- Am I satisfied with the balance between the time I invest in my professional relationships versus the time spent with friends and family?
- What if all of my clients disappeared tomorrow? Do I have enough relationships with other types of people that I could, with their help, rapidly rebuild my client base?

Systematically develop your relationship capital, and you'll have an asset that is even more valuable to you than your retirement savings.

6 | Benjamin Franklin's Secret Weapon

In 1721, the printer James Franklin launched a newspaper called the *New England Courant*. James hated the conservative Boston religious establishment of the time, in particular the prominent, arch-conservative, fire-and-brimstone preacher Cotton Mather. He lashed out at Mather in acerbic editorials, and Mather didn't hesitate to counterattack. Under fictitious names, James also published articles and letters attacking Mather. One morning, to his delight, a well-crafted, humorous letter appeared under his door written by "Silence Dogood"—a pseudonym, unknown to James, adopted by his sixteen-year-old brother Benjamin, who had served as his apprentice since the age of twelve.

Whereas James made direct attacks on public figures in his articles and editorials, Silence Dogood used prodding humor and irony to satirize everything from Harvard University to Boston politicians. A few months later, James was arrested and jailed, ostensibly for refusing to reveal his journalistic sources but most likely for his scathing public criticisms. He left Benjamin, at the age of a typical tenth-grader today, as the editor and publisher of the *Courant*.

Ben Franklin had learned his lesson: Humor and indirect questioning produced many friends and few enemies, while drawing attention to the important issues. He later wrote about his "indirect method":

> I was charmed with it, adopted it, dropped my abrupt contradiction, and positive argumentation, and put on the humble inquirer and doubter. . . . I practiced it continually and grew very artful and expert in drawing people even of superior knowledge into concessions the consequences of which they did not foresee.[1]

This was only one of many qualities that made Franklin a master at building relationship capital. It might not have been so. As biographer H. W. Brands writes in *The First American,* "Genius is prone to producing envy. Yet it was part of Franklin's genius that he produced far less than his share, due to an unusual ability to disarm those disposed to envy." He adds that Franklin "learned to deflect credit for some of his most important inventions. He avoided arguments altogether. Laughing, his opponents listened and were persuaded."[2]

Benjamin's brother James was eventually released from jail, and the younger Franklin decided he could no longer abide by the near-slave status that characterized an apprenticeship in the eighteenth century. At the age of seventeen, Benjamin ran away from Boston and went to Philadelphia, where he hoped to make his fortune. He arrived in the state capital in 1723, penniless and disheveled after weeks of travel. It was soon apparent that Franklin was highly adept at building relationships with influential individuals who would later help his career. His broad intellect and range of knowledge—Franklin had always been an avid reader—were unusual for a seventeen-year-old, and adults invariably found him an interesting, curious, and engaging individual. People liked Franklin as soon as they met him, and they usually wanted to get to know him better.

A cousin of Franklin's, Robert Homes, wrote to him from Delaware, asking him to return to his family in Boston. Franklin wrote a careful letter back to Homes, thoughtfully explaining his motivations for leaving Boston and describing how happy he was to be in Philadelphia. The provincial governor of Pennsylvania, William Keith, who happened to be with Homes when he received the letter, read it and was amazed to learn that the author of such an articulate letter was so young. He knew that Philadelphia had hardly any good printers and decided to seek out this young man and encourage him to set up shop.

Keith went to visit one of only two printing shops in Philadelphia, and coincidentally found Franklin working there as a part-time helper. The owner of the shop was flabbergasted as the governor of his province grabbed Franklin, whom he knew only from his thoughtful letter, and took him off for a glass of port at a nearby tavern. Finding him even more impressive in the flesh than on paper, Keith agreed to help him start his own printing business. Although Keith later let young Franklin down when he went to London to buy printing equipment, the story illustrates how people were *drawn* to Franklin, who later went on to become the leading printer in the American colonies.

Another quality that endeared Franklin to everyone who came into contact with him was his focus on ideas and relationships rather than money. Some of us may think of Franklin as the prototypical American capitalist, and while he was an enormously successful businessman, making money was never his primary objective. As Brands puts it, "For Franklin the getting of money was always a means to an end, never the end itself."[3] Once he got his printing business up and running, his energies turned elsewhere—to politics, scientific invention, and other pursuits. In 1740, for example, Franklin invented the free-standing wood stove—then called the "Pennsylvania fireplace," today known as the Franklin stove. This marvelous invention greatly reduced the amount of wood required to keep a house warm in the winter (fireplaces are notoriously inefficient for heating a room, due to loss of heat up the chimney). The governor of Pennsylvania offered Franklin the exclusive rights to sell his new fireplace in the province, an arrangement that would have made Franklin a very wealthy man, but he refused. "That as we enjoy great advantages from the inventions of others," he wrote, "we should be glad of an opportunity to serve others by any invention of ours, and this we should do freely and generously."[4]

Franklin went on to an illustrious career. He was an extraordinarily successful inventor, and probably the individual most responsible for the American colonies' victory over Britain in their war for independence—Franklin's successful efforts to convince the French to support the colonies helped turn the tide against the overwhelmingly superior British forces. After the Revolutionary War, he was the guiding hand at the convention where the new constitution was crafted.

It was Benjamin Franklin's ability to build relationship capital, however, which is of particular relevance to modern business professionals. Although extraordinarily bright, Franklin was self-effacing. He was also *interesting*—he was well read and a great conversationalist—and all of these qualities combined into an appealing whole that attracted others to him and helped him to establish relationships immediately. Furthermore, his indirect, humorous means of getting his points across endeared him even to his few ostensible enemies. As a result, Franklin had an abundance of the different types of relationship capital outlined in the previous chapter—catalysts, like Governor William Keith, who made key introductions for him in Philadelphia; collaborators or business partners, many of whom joined Franklin in the various printing businesses he founded; and clients, who were drawn to his publications by virtue of his high-quality writing and printing. Franklin was also brilliant at all four of the phases of building relationship capital—affiliating, adding value, sustaining, and multiplying. Publishing your ideas, for example, is a powerful way to multiply your influence, and Franklin honed his writing abilities from a young age. Later, through his printing and publishing endeavors, he ensured that he always had a public outlet for his thinking.

In 1790, Benjamin Franklin died at the age of eighty-four with his family and friends at his side. He was a man of solid material riches, but more important, he was beloved and admired on two continents. He faced his own death with the same calmness and equanimity he had demonstrated throughout his life, even joking, when told that by shifting his position in bed he would breath more easily, that "a dying man can do nothing *easy!*" Over 20,000 Philadelphians turned out for his funeral.

Franklin also wanted to influence future generations. As a youth he had been staked several loans to begin his first printing business, and he wanted to offer the same support to other young men and women. He therefore left £2,000 in a special fund, split between Boston and Philadelphia, that would provide small, low-interest loans to up-and-coming professionals who had finished their apprenticeships. Two hundred years later, in 1990, the funds were worth $4.5 million and $2.0 million, respectively, and to this day they continue to provide scholarships for worthy students.

Benjamin Franklin was America's counterpart to Italy's Leonardo da Vinci, the Renaissance genius whom you'll read about in Chapter 9. Apprenticed at an early age, neither man received a formal education. Self-taught outside their trades (printer and artist, respectively), they both made indelible marks in history. Whereas Leonardo was an irascible, prickly genius, Franklin—no less intelligent—exemplified the consummate relationship builder. He knew how smart he was but rarely let it show. He had many of the answers but preferred to ask provocative questions. Although he quickly discerned others' faults, he allowed them to discover them for themselves through his humor and indirect approach. He was one of the most knowledgeable men on the planet, but his insatiable curiosity and zest for learning new things never flagged.

Not a bad approach for building client relationships in the twenty-first century.

7 | Why a Client Might Like You

In a letter penned to her sister on Christmas Eve in 1798, the English novelist Jane Austen wrote, "I do not want people to be very agreeable, as it saves me the trouble of liking them a great deal."[1] On the face of it, this is a rather odd statement. Austen was an extraordinarily astute observer of human nature, however, and in her letter she hints at something quite relevant for twenty-first-century professionals: When we like someone, we are inclined to help them and develop a relationship with them. Although it's hard to know today exactly what Austen was thinking when she made this statement, I can't help but believe she clearly recognized the obligation that liking someone can bring.

In business, we are generally motivated to build long-term relationships with people who can help us reach our goals *and* whom we like. This is not always true in our personal lives, but that's a different story. Sometimes we have neurotic reasons for associating with someone, and it has nothing do with liking them.

If we don't like someone, we may do business with him, but he'll be a vendor who never becomes part of our inner circle. Then, if competitors offer a product or service that's just as good, and we also *like them,* there's a good chance we'll switch suppliers. It's that simple. What's not so simple is precisely why we like some people and not others. What genuine behaviors and attitudes spur a client's interest in getting to know us and wanting to work with us? Let's explore the roots of likability and see how you can put your best foot forward, so to speak, each time you meet a new client—or anyone, for that matter.

In 1936, Dale Carnegie wrote *How to Win Friends and Influence People.* In his book, he sets out a series of principles that we can employ to encourage others to like us. They include: Be interested in others; smile; use first names; be a good listener; talk in terms of others' interests; and make people feel important.[2] In many ways, Carnegie is right on the mark. Since he wrote this book, however, there has been a great deal of scientific research done on why we like people. Furthermore, today's clients are relatively sophisticated and are unlikely to be easily swayed by a smile or because they're addressed by their first name.

Drawing on the interviews I have conducted with corporate executives and individual clients over many years, as well as ideas developed by Robert Cialdini in *Influence: The Psychology of Persuasion,* I propose the following framework of six major factors that influence whether and to what extent we like someone at a first meeting.

1. Similarity

A law firm bids for a large assignment and is chosen over half a dozen other competitors. Did this group of lawyers win because they were perceived as having better legal expertise? No, the client views the top three bidders as being equal on this score. So what pushes this plum contract their way? One of the lead attorneys lists "polo" on her resume under recreation, and, you guessed it, the in-house counsel choosing outside lawyers also plays polo, a somewhat esoteric and rarified pastime. Unfair? No, human nature—we like people with whom we have things in common.

This principle applies to even banal similarities. A study done in the 1970s, for example, had young people go onto a college campus and ask students for a dime to make a phone call. When the experimenters were dressed in a similar fashion to the students, the request was granted more than two-thirds of the time; when they were dressed differently, the success rate was far lower.[3] Other studies have shown that we are more inclined to sign a petition if we perceive the petitioner to be similar to ourselves in dress and appearance.[4]

From a practical standpoint, it's important to find commonalities and connection points with clients. These could include just about anything: family status (you both have teenage children, or perhaps a newborn baby), education (you went to the same school or had the same major in college), sports (you played Jai-Alai in college, too?), or just about any other shared experience. If I meet a client from Minnesota, I would probably bring up my month-long experience at the Minnesota Outward Bound School located near the Minnesota/Canada border. I might ask a potential client if he has any favorite business book authors—perhaps I know one of them personally, and suddenly there is another point of intersection.

The objective is to find and explore *genuine* areas of common interest. Insincerity or ingratiating behavior is usually patently obvious and even repulsive to clients.

2. Familiarity

I have a rule of thumb that rarely fails me and has successfully been used by many other professionals: If you are making a proposal to a new client, the more face-to-face meetings you have, the more likely you are to win the business. This sounds obvious, but many people don't follow it—they meet once or twice with a client and then fire off a proposal.

Simply put, we like things we are familiar with. I remember a comment an Italian friend made to me about restaurants in Rome: "New restaurants in this city almost always fail. Italians like familiar places with familiar faces, and they just stick to their habitual restaurants where they are treated extremely well." We are all a bit like that, actually. We gravitate toward familiar foods, familiar surroundings, and familiar people. The more contact a client has with us, the more she can get a sense for personal chemistry, trustworthiness, personal values, and integrity. Occasionally it doesn't work out—some people just aren't very compatible—but in general familiarity creates an advantage over the competition.

3. Positive Association

I once made an appearance on CNBC News to talk about building long-term client relationships, and on the air the interviewer said to me, tongue-in-cheek, "Well, we see that some of your clients have included Citibank and American Express, and that's of course why we wanted you on the show!" In fact, she didn't realize how true that statement, said in jest, really was. If a person is associated with something or someone that we like or respect, a transference occurs and we are more inclined to also like that person. That's why corporations pay millions of dollars to celebrities to endorse their products: Through positive association with a movie or rock star we adore, they hope that we will like and then buy their products.

So how do you make positive association work for you? First of all, as a general principle it means you always have to be discerning about whom you associate with, because clients—like others—will judge you by the company you keep. To the extent you have worked for some admired or blue-chip clients, either individuals or corporations, make that known up-front. Have you been published in a reputable journal or been interviewed by a well-known TV network personality, radio announcer, or journalist? Have you ever had the opportunity to work with a respected corporate executive, academic, or accomplished public figure? Be sure to communicate this experience to potential clients.

4. Praising What's Good

Numerous studies have shown that we feel more positively toward people when they give us compliments, even if we know the statements are untrue.[5] In other words, we like people who *praise* us and whom we believe *like us*; conversely, no one enjoys criticism. Dale Carnegie points out that even the most hardened criminals, when confronted with their crimes, feel unjustly attacked and misunderstood. "Under my coat is a weary heart, but a kind one—one that would do nobody harm," a famous mobster in the 1930s proclaimed—with complete sincerity—to the police after he was finally arrested after years of committing mayhem and murder.[6]

Joe Girard, who is listed in the *Guinness Book of World Records* as the world's greatest car salesman, exemplifies this principle put to practical use. He sold an average of five cars a day and earned a hefty six-figure income. His secret? "A fair price and someone they like to buy from."[7] Apparently, he sent every one of his 13,000 former customers a card *every month of the year*—146,000 cards in total. And what did those cards say? Simply, "I like you."

These research findings are fascinating, but I don't mean to suggest that you throw away the objectivity and independence you must show as a client advisor and become an insincere flatterer. The lesson is that we must accentuate the positive as well as the negative. It's just as important to tell clients what they're doing right—both at an institutional level and on a personal level—as it is to pick apart their performance. When I conduct a series of executive interviews at the beginning of an assignment, for example, I always begin my report to management with what's working well. I also try to give individual clients positive feedback about their performance as executives. Remember that senior executives don't necessarily get a lot of praise and positive feedback from their own organizations. They are constantly confronted by problems they have to solve, and their boss isn't usually spending a lot of time telling them how well they're doing. A word of encouragement from a trusted outsider can be welcome and motivating.

I recently introduced a friend to my own financial advisors, Mallory White and Carl Luff of Raymond James, and asked them to review his portfolio. I sent my friend to them because, frankly, his investments were a complete mess and I knew it. When Mallory and Carl prepared their initial analysis of his portfolio, I was braced for a scathing assessment. I could just hear them saying, "It's the worst we've ever seen," and then pinching their noses in disgust. Instead, they started with the positives: "The bonds in the portfolio are really terrific," Mallory said as she began the conversation. "You've done a great job putting that part of your investments together. You've also made some excellent stock picks that are very appropriate for your age and financial situation." Then, they pointed out the shortcomings and weaknesses. I remember feeling relief but also an enhanced sense of trust in these advisors—they weren't completely trashing my friend's investments in an attempt to persuade him to hire them.

5. Openness

At a client meeting recently, a best-selling author who was a respected expert in his field made frequent allusions to past clients and investment situations, but cloaked them in vague language and inscrutable insinuations. I felt as if I were talking to a CIA agent. His answers were always a bit evasive, and it was clear that he wasn't going to reveal much information until he was on the client's payroll. Later, I discovered that while clients hired him to speak at corporate conferences, they rarely followed up and used him for consultation. He was a closed book, and because of that, clients didn't particularly like him or feel inclined to build a relationship with him.

In contrast, my colleague William Wallace, whose story I told in the Introduction, has always had an openness that is highly inviting to anyone he meets. Everything about his demeanor says, "This guy has nothing to hide." Not surprisingly, since leaving consulting, William has had a successful career as an entrepreneur and now as a top corporate executive in his job as president of a major division of Verizon.

The quality of openness is very appealing to clients. Here are some of the factors that convey such an attitude:

- *Body language.* Successful advisors practice looking a client in the eye, shaking her hand firmly, maintaining an open, erect posture when sitting at a table, appearing interested in what a client has to say, but not fawning and gushing over every word.
- *A willingness to share.* There is a school of thought that until a client is actually paying you, you shouldn't reveal too much information. I think this is bunk. The more you share with a client up-front, the more he will be inclined to hire you. Wouldn't you be more enthusiastic about hiring a financial advisor if, during your first hour with her, she gave you good insights about your issues and provided some valuable information?
- *Honesty.* When clients ask you tough questions, do you beat around the bush or do you just give them an honest answer? Whenever I am asked a difficult question, I always try to follow up with another question to understand what's important to the client. So if a client asks, "Have you ever worked in the specialty chemicals industry before?" I answer honestly—but I then inquire, "What are you looking for in an outside resource?" or "How much industry experience do you think is necessary?"

6. Rapport

To some extent, a general sense of rapport is the result of many of these behaviors. But there is a particular aspect of rapport that deserves a separate discussion, and that is the specific feeling on the part of clients that we are *in sync with them.* This feeling will be based on the extent to which we are matching our client along a number of dimensions, including voice, gestures, style, and content. For example, rapport will be enhanced if you match your client in:

- Pacing the conversation.
- Degree of formality or informality.

- Pitch and tone of your voice.
- Body language.
- Energy level.
- Orientation toward people as opposed to the task.
- Dress.
- Personal space.
- Degree to which you are fact-based rather than merely anecdotal.

In practical terms, if a client is informal, enjoys talking about things outside of work, and has a sense of humor, respond in kind and you'll start to develop rapport. If you compensate by constantly redirecting the conversation to business issues, the client will have a vague sense of being out of sync—of just not relating to you.

Don't be artificial or insincere, but do your best to relate to clients in a way that maximizes their receptiveness to your ideas and the possibility of a personal relationship rather than just an arm's-length transaction.

These same principles of likability, by the way, apply to any situation where you are meeting someone new. A friend of mine recently interviewed for the top job at a major hospital, for example, and before he went for the first round of interviews, I walked him through these six behaviors. A highly educated doctor, he was very concerned with thoroughly communicating his medical credentials and experience. As a result of our practice interviews, he focused on finding similarities and commonalities with the senior medical staff interviewing him, first praising them for what he saw as the strengths of their hospital, but then honestly critiquing the hospital's shortcomings. He presented his accomplishments, mentioning several respected individuals he had worked with in the medical profession; and he was sensitive to his interviewers' pacing, tone, and body language. He reported to me afterward that in just a few hours he established a degree of rapport with his interlocutors that on other occasions had taken days to build. Not surprisingly, he got the job.

8

The Myth of Meeting Client Expectations

"Identify and then meet or exceed your client's expectations!" This exhortation has become the accepted wisdom about how to excel with clients. It is indeed a useful axiom—that is, if you see your role as that of an expert for hire. If you aspire to be a *client advisor* who builds long-term loyalty, however, it is a dangerously limiting and even misleading piece of advice. Consider these examples of client relationships gone sour:

- A shipping company retained a major consulting firm and asked it to help improve the efficiency of its operations. The senior partner in charge of the engagement delegated most of the work to a team of bright young associates whose insightful analytic work identified profit improvement opportunities that exceeded the client's stated goals. Halfway through the project, however, the client's CEO called the partner and abruptly cancelled the work for unspecified reasons. Six months later, a friend of the CEO told the consulting firm that the CEO had anticipated a one-on-one counseling relationship with the senior partner, but it had never materialized—"I got this team of young MBAs instead," he complained.

- An advertising agency designed an effective set of commercials that resulted in meaningful sales increases of the client's product. When the campaign was over, the client put the account out to bid, saying that it had a policy of periodically looking at other agencies for good ideas. In fact, the client's vice president of marketing didn't like several key members of the agency's team and felt the overall personal chemistry was poor. He wanted an agency that was more enjoyable to work with.

These are true and not atypical anecdotes about professionals who got canned even though they met and even exceeded clearly stated and formally negotiated client expectations. So what's up here? How do we cross this minefield called "client expectations"?

Here are four principles that will provide you with the broadest possible palette for adding value to your clients:

1. *Clients always have hidden or unarticulated expectations that have nothing to do with quantitative business objectives.* In the first example, the client's CEO thought he was buying a relationship with a highly experienced partner who was going to provide a forum to bounce around big-picture ideas about his business. Yet even a thorough and questioning proposal development process failed to uncover this assumption. In the second example, the client wanted, in addition to good ads, a warm, enjoyable, personal relationship with his agency staff. In neither case would these expectations ever have been stated out loud, and in any event they were ignored until the consulting firm or ad agency was fired.

Client *advisors* focus as much on the qualitative, personal aspects of the business relationship as they do on meeting stated operational goals, and they have the sensitivity to recognize them even when the client cannot or will not express them. Sometimes there are client expectations that are simply *unknowable*. This is why principle 2, that follows, is so important—you won't always be able to grasp every one of your client's expectations, and so you have to take a broad focus on improving his business in ways he has asked as well as in ways he hasn't even expressed.

2. *Most professionals define "expectations" and "client" too narrowly.* A CEO I once worked for referred me to a far-flung division within his company, ostensibly to do the same type of strategy development effort that I had successfully completed for him. The division head, indeed, wanted a new approach to the market. The CEO, however, was hoping I would instigate a cultural change—a mind-set shift—among the division executives, something I discerned only over a long dinner punctuated by several bottles of French Burgundy (I took a taxi home). Suddenly my task was much more complicated, and meeting my new client's expectations (a revitalized market strategy for the division) alone would have constituted failure in the mind of the CEO.

Your "client," in the broadest sense, is far more than the executive who hired you. It could include a more senior executive you've never even met, a young up-and-coming manager who is part of a team you're working with, or the spouse or grown children of your client if you advise individuals.

3. *Improving your client's condition, not just meeting expectations, is paramount.* I have a current client who asked me to design and facilitate a quarterly strategy meeting offsite with his senior management team. I have done that, and the sessions have been extremely successful (I am not advocating that you dodge expected deliverables in favor of something else—I take the client's explicit goals very seriously). In between these sessions, however, I have added significant value, including introducing my client to a potential strategic partner, coaching two senior executives on their managerial style, and helping the CEO prepare his year-end evaluation for his board of directors. These value-added activities were not part of the client's

stated—or even hidden—expectations for this assignment. Yet if you asked the CEO about the value of my work, he would cite these latter contributions as being just as important as the workshops we formally contracted for.

Some readers may be wondering if they should be compensated for such extra services. The short answer is "Yes, but it may not always happen." You have three choices here: Price them in at the beginning; negotiate them as additions to your contract; or give some of them away, especially the ones that are high value but take up little time.

4. *Tell your client, tactfully, about how you've helped her.* If you've been married or had a partner for more than a year or so, chances are that individual does things for you that you are already taking for granted. The same thing happens in professional-client relationships. Whereas in a close, romantic relationship it is tacky and even neurotic to recite all of your contributions to the partnership (we rely on each other to reach out and recognize them), it is often appropriate and indeed necessary to do it in business. Some clients are great at recognizing your value, but others are so preoccupied with running their businesses that they don't really add it all up.

You can elegantly highlight the value you have provided in several ways: First, you can sit down and periodically review your performance with your client, and in that session both give and solicit comments about your contributions as well as about what you could do better. Second, you can encourage *others* in the organization to give your principal client feedback about your contributions. Remember, third-party endorsements are far more powerful than anything we say about ourselves. So when a manager in your client's organization tells you how much she enjoys working with you or expresses gratitude for your contributions—by all means encourage her to tell that directly to your client. The turning point in the relationship with one of my own clients came when a subordinate told him, "I don't know how much we're paying Sobel for his work, but whatever it is, he's worth far more his fees." (I'd like to tell you that *every* client of mine says this about me, but that would be a lie. Maybe they *think* it without saying it out loud. . . .) When an executive hears this from one of his managers, it is very powerful.

Rethink what you're trying to do for your clients. Experts for hire and "steady suppliers" merely try to identify and then meet or exceed their clients' expectations—a level of performance that often keeps them employed. Great advisors, in contrast, look for myriad ways to improve their clients' business condition, and they help the individuals they serve become better managers and better people. This success enables them to become part of their client's inner circle.

Which kind of professional—expert for hire or long-term advisor—do *you* aspire to become?

9 | Leonardo da Vinci

Why Lutes and Madonnas Matter

In 1481, at the age of thirty, the Italian artist Leonardo da Vinci left Florence and moved to Milan in search of a patron or client. While living in Florence, he had completed his apprenticeship to Andrea Verrocchio and established his early reputation as a brilliant and original painter. Florence had an abundance of artistic talent, however, and the competition for patrons—wealthy rulers or noblemen who could afford to give out commissions for works of art—was intense. Milan lacked Florence's artistic resources, so Leonardo headed to a city where he had a greater chance of establishing his own base of loyal patrons.

When Leonardo arrived in Milan, he brought with him a rare lute he had constructed in the shape of a horse's head. (In addition to being an accomplished painter, he was also a skilled lutenist.) Milanese high society was apparently quite taken by his musical talents and his unusual instrument, and the social contacts he developed as a result of his hobnobbing—not unlike some modern consultants or bankers—turned out to be instrumental in procuring art commissions.

Eyeing his ideal client, Leonardo drafted a letter offering his services to the Milanese ruler Ludovico Sforza: "I offer to execute, at your convenience, all of the items briefly noted below." The extraordinary list consists almost entirely of descriptions of innovative military inventions that could be put at Sforza's service. "I have a model of very strong but light bridges, extremely easy to carry. . . . During a siege, I know how to dry up the water of the moats. . . . I have models of mortars that are easy to transport. . . . I will make covered vehicles, safe and unassailable, which will penetrate enemy ranks . . ." and so on. The list is amazingly prescient—it describes many military inventions that didn't come into mainstream use until centuries later. Interestingly, only at the very end of this letter does Leonardo mention putting his prodigious artistic talents to work for the Milanese leader, saying, "Moreover, [a] bronze horse could be made that will be to the immortal glory and honor of the lord your father."[1]

Why did Leonardo, an artist who had no particular experience in designing or building weapons, position himself to Sforza as a military engineer? The answer is quite simple: In 1482, most of the Italian city-states were on a war footing—the Turks had invaded southern Italy, and Venice had hired Swiss mercenaries and was threatening Milan. Sforza was being inexorably drawn into the conflict. Leonardo, no slouch, was adjusting his service offering to his client's presumed needs at the time. Sforza needed ideas about how to wage war, not altarpieces with depictions of the Virgin Mary. The ever-creative Leonardo emphasized his inventive engineering skills rather than his artistic abilities.

Great client advisors have both depth and breadth, and Leonardo da Vinci was an example of a consummate *deep generalist*. An illegitimate child who grew up in a small town in Tuscany, Leonardo had virtually no formal education. When he was brought to Florence and apprenticed to Verrocchio at age 15, he knew nothing of Latin and probably could barely read. Although he lacked education,

Leonardo rarely failed to master whatever discipline or task he set himself to. At his death, he had become one of the most accomplished artists in history. He had designed hundreds of inventions, including a water-powered alarm clock, a parachute, a variable-intensity table lamp, and a helicopter—all of them well before their time. Moreover, he created anatomical studies that were unequaled for nearly three hundred years. Leonardo was simply fascinated by everything around him, writing, "The desire to know is natural to good men."

Leonardo's own humble origins clearly shaped his approach to learning and his philosophy of education. First of all, he believed that imitation was a waste of time. "The painter will produce mediocre pictures," he wrote, "if he is inspired by the work of others." Artists and scientists, he felt, should base their work on direct observation and analysis. Leonard exemplified an important trait of great learners—he got his hands dirty! He valued hands-on learning rather than academic study, perhaps a reaction to the fact that he found himself keeping company with highly literate Renaissance scholars who quoted left and right from recently discovered Greek and Latin texts. He wrote, "Anyone who invokes authors in a discussion is not using his intelligence but his memory." His studies of human anatomy, for example, are based on hundreds of hours spent dissecting corpses—not a common activity in Renaissance Italy!

Many of the modern professionals I have interviewed talk about the need to get deeply involved with the nuts and bolts of your relationships, no matter how senior you are, to experience the client's situation and issues first hand. Former General Electric chief executive Jack Welch calls it "diving deep"—he once spent an entire week with Wal-Mart founder Sam Walton, for example, in an effort to understand why his retail chain was so successful. Abraham Lincoln, as a young lawyer, similarly "dived deep" by riding the Eighth Judicial Circuit for three months each year across the state of Illinois. He traveled by horse with a judge and other lawyers, working with clients in dozens of small towns across 11,000 square miles of rural countryside. Despite the hardship—sometimes Lincoln would sleep in a hotel room with a dozen other men—he accumulated a wealth of practical experience and knowledge through his exposure to so many different clients and legal issues, most of which had to be resolved in a few days. "Getting his hands dirty" yielded another benefit: He built relationships with thousands of voters who later supported his political career.

Leonardo also put great emphasis on inventiveness, which, according to some historians, explains why he actually painted so few works. Writes one biographer, "He was incapable of repeating what had already been done by someone else, and only took up his brushes once a revolution in the mind had been accomplished."[2] He developed a innovative technique in his early paintings, for example, that involved carefully applying many fine layers of thin paint over a primed surface, resulting in a mysterious luminosity created by the light as it passed through the surface layers and was reflected back. When he painted the famous Last Supper, he completely broke with convention, and instead of placing Judas off to the side without a halo (the custom among Renaissance painters), he placed him close to Christ and on the right, differentiating him with nuances of expression and shadow. Leonardo designed a 24-foot bronze horse for Ludovico Sforza, and because of its great height, had to invent an entirely new way of casting bronze. Unfortunately, his client was drawn into a war on the eve of the casting, and Sforza's army requisitioned the 72 tons of bronze that had been accumulated for the statue and used it to make cannonballs and artillery shells.

Leonardo's most famous employer was the vicious, despotic Cesare Borgia, who ruled over Milan with an iron fist. One biographer writes, "The two men must have taken an instant liking to each other. The boldness of the artist-engineer corresponded in some ways to the audacity of the prince. . . . [T]hese two bastard children respected each other for their intelligence, independence of mind, and scorn for convention."[3] Borgia hired Leonardo as his chief military engineer, and Leonardo spent many months touring the battlefields of northern Italy, acting as a consultant on how to improve fortifications and drain swampy land. Interestingly, during this time Leonardo met Niccolò Machiavelli, who had been sent by the Florentine government to observe Borgia's operations up close. The two hit it off and spent many late nights in deep conversation about the world's problems—who wouldn't want to have been a fly on the wall during one of those sessions! Within a year, Leonardo left Borgia's service; whether he became fed up with Borgia's ruthless style and walked away or simply moved to greener pastures is hard to tell.

Leonardo was highly trained as a master artist, but he branched out into many other disciplines. He constantly went to the source for his learning, studying the ripples in a pond with the same intensity he had for the subjects of his paintings such as the Mona Lisa. He was not satisfied with imitation but rather insisted on bringing something new and different to all of his creations. He also challenged conventional wisdom—he took nothing for granted, and constantly questioned why things were done a certain way, whether it was the traditional technique of applying paint to a canvas (he invented his own style) or the accepted way of swaddling newborn infants (they were wrapped far too tightly, he asserted). Even in his sixties, near the end of his life, Leonardo was busy studying new areas of science, and cooking up more projects than ever—one of his last proposed inventions was a huge parabolic mirror that could be used to harness solar power to use in the dying of textiles.

Although Leonardo was clearly born with innate genius, his learning habits—which anyone can emulate—are relevant for modern professionals. There are six important learning arenas that you need to focus on in order to evolve from a narrow specialist to a deep generalist:

1. *Yourself.* Self-knowledge is the starting point for your learning journey. Self-knowledge is absolutely necessary for empathy, and honest self-appraisal provides you with insight into your intellectual and emotional strengths and weaknesses. Leonardo kept detailed journals his entire life, recording daily events but also reflecting on his perceptions and his moods—a technique, interestingly,

advocated by some modern psychotherapists as a means of getting in touch with ourselves.

2. *Your core specialty.* You've got to be top-flight at your core expertise. It's your ticket to admission as far as getting the attention of new clients, and you need to continually develop it during your entire career. Leonardo himself, despite his precocious and prodigious natural talent, spent nearly 15 years as an apprentice to the Florentine master Andrea Verrocchio. Even as he branched out into new areas like anatomy and engineering, he continued to refine and develop his painting skills for the rest of his life.

3. *Your personal interests.* Ideally, work is play, but most of us have interests that go beyond our chosen professional focus. Your personal interests—whether they include collecting antiques, playing the piano, scuba diving, biking, or something else altogether—have a way of combining with your professional learning to create a balanced whole. They subtly influence your perspectives and make you a more interesting person to your clients. It was Leonardo's lute playing, for example, that first established him in Milan and enabled him to network with wealthy aristocrats.

4. *Your personal knowledge of your client.* The better you know your client personally, the more effective you will be at advising him and tailoring your services to his needs. You'll have a clearer understanding of how to go the extra mile and add value beyond your what is specified in your written contract. You'll also become more adept at tailoring your communications style to your client's particular personality type. Personal knowledge and familiarity, as we have seen, are also critical for building trust.

5. *Your client's organization.* Just as Leonardo spent months trudging around the freezing countryside to study Cesare Borgia's fortifications and encampments, you need to develop intimate knowledge of your client's organization, her strategy, and her

operations. Insights about your client's business emerge when you combine your own experiences with deep client knowledge.

6. *Your client's industry and environment.* You can't be very useful to your client if you don't have a thorough understanding of the industry and the overall business ecosystem that he lives in. This is why, for example, many professional service firms and corporations have developed a marketing focus on industry segments or "vertical markets." A strong knowledge of industry trends and practices, an understanding of what's going on with our economy, and a more general feel for management trends and ideas all form an important backdrop to the specific client issues you are working on.

Learning Journeys: *Client and Self*

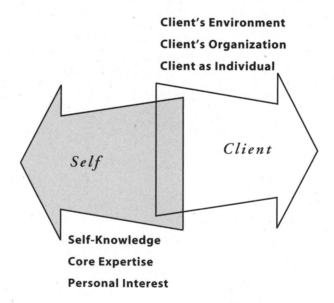

In our culture, we tend to revere experts—individuals who have an enormous depth of knowledge in one area. As the half-life of knowledge shrinks, however, we have to question the very concept of acquiring "expertise" that then serves us for the rest of our lives. A college or graduate education should teach us how to think logically and how to learn going forward, not dump a body of soon-to-be obsolete knowledge into our brains. As one historian says about Leonardo, "He had not been to a university. He learned through chance meetings, by observation, or by reading and asking questions."[4] Leonardo used to refer to himself as "a disciple of experience." Not a bad approach once you've finished your formal education.

I picture Leonardo as an old man, physically weak but as excited as ever about his latest project or his newest discovery. He sits on the seashore, resting, but his ever-sharp mind focuses on the incoming surf and the shifting tide, speculating about the nature of wave energy. He stares at a seashell and pockets it, thinking it might make a good design for a staircase. He makes a few notes in his handwritten lexicon, which already contains nine thousand words.

Leonardo da Vinci passed away nearly 500 years ago, but he's still an inspirational role model for twenty-first century learners!

10

Finding the Hidden Creases

Influencing Your Clients

Physical labor is often a fundamental part of Zen training. During his studies with a famous Zen archery master in Hawaii, Kenneth Kushner found himself engaged in the arduous task of moving large rocks to make way for a new footpath. A psychotherapist by training, Kushner found it nearly impossible to dislodge the heavy boulders, and he was quickly exhausted by his futile efforts. In his book *One Arrow, One Life,* he writes about an important lesson he learned from his Zen teacher:

> Tanouye Roshi watched me with considerable amusement. He explained I was trying to impose my will on the rocks; I was trying to make them go where I wanted them to go. "You have to learn to push the rock where it wants to go," he explained to me. He explained further that, if I could do that, I could coax the rocks to where I wanted them to go. He then showed me that, because the rocks are unevenly shaped, there is usually one direction in which, if pushed, the rock is easier to unbalance and flip over. He told me that I must learn how to utilize the

direction in which the rock "wanted" to go in order to move it
where I wanted it to go. . . . He continued to demonstrate how,
by repeating the process of pushing the rock in its favored direction and occasionally spinning the rock so as to reorient the
direction it "wanted" to go, it was quite easy to move it where
I wanted it to go.[1]

Influencing clients is very similar to moving boulders. All of
your clients will have in mind a direction *they* wish to take, and you
will naturally try to persuade them to follow *your* direction. This
is true whether you're a consultant, a public relations professional,
or a salesperson trying to convince a client to place an order for
your products. A client's favored direction could be thought of as a
"hidden crease"—he will be predisposed to moving that way, just
as a piece of paper will easily fold again where it has been previously
creased. The Zen approach to life is to find the hidden creases in
every activity—the "naturally correct" way of doing things, as
Kushner says.

You don't have to become a Zen Buddhist to influence clients,
but this principle has relevance to professional-client relationships.
The best strategy with clients is not to bludgeon them into taking
your advice but rather to understand where they want to go and
then influence their trajectory 10 or 20 degrees at a time. As Ben
Franklin said, "If you would persuade, you must appeal to interest
rather than intellect."[2]

I once had a client who was dead set on promoting a certain
executive to a position I felt he was completely inappropriate for.
Not only did he lack the skills for the job, but his promotion and
ostensibly closer relationship with my client threatened to send a
bad signal to the broader organization. When I first raised my objections, it was like trying to move one of the heavy boulders that
stymied Kenneth Kushner in the previous story—my client was set
in his direction.

My next line of attack was to spin my client on his axis ever
so slightly: I suggested I help him develop the detailed roles and

responsibilities for the new position. Since this client was a Baby Boomer—we'll explore the implications of this later in the chapter—he was very comfortable creating detailed documentation around the new position, something that an older executive from the Traditionalist generation might have resisted. We did this, and I successfully began to orient the new role more toward internal coordination rather than working externally with clients, something this individual was very weak at. Next, we worked on the reporting relationships for this executive—should he report directly to my client, who was the division head, or to my client's chief of staff?

My client had long complained about not having enough time for his role as strategist and visionary leader of the business, and I emphasized this to him in debating the right reporting structure. I also appealed to his desire to shake things up in his business unit—again, a typical characteristic of Baby Boomers who wanted to change the establishment in the 1960s and still do. Furthermore, I got the chief of staff to pull him aside and argue why this new executive should report to him rather than my client. Again, I was moving my client in a direction he wanted to go—more time for strategic thinking and leadership—but also in a direction I felt he should go. At the end of this process, the client felt he had made great progress, and I was satisfied that I had moved him in the right direction and done the best I could for him and his organization.

Because I have a bit of a stubborn streak, sometimes I have wanted to say to my wife, "Before you say anything, let me structure the nature of your advice so that I can accept it!" My urge illustrates a fundamental point: Part of the art of working with clients is understanding how best to communicate effectively and persuade them. And practicing that art depends on how well you can understand clients' hidden creases.

A case-in-point is John Balkcom, who took over as president of St. John's College after a distinguished career in business, including a long stint as a partner at consultants Booz, Allen &

Hamilton. St. John's, with twin campuses in Annapolis and Santa Fe, has a unique curriculum that teaches the great books. Despite possessing several degrees, including a master's degree in the classics from St. John's itself, Balkcom does not have the typical pedigree of a college president—that is, he does not hold a PhD and cannot claim long experience in teaching in a university setting.

When he first arrived, Balkcom—like any good strategic consultant—thought about the need to develop a new strategy for St. John's. After meeting at length with his faculty, however, some of whom have taught at St. John's for over 30 years, he changed his mind—he realized it was not a good idea to immediately propose major changes in direction to an institution whose strength is teaching the classics to students in small discussion groups. Instead of advocating a grand vision or strategy, he formed three "college committees," led by experienced faculty, to examine three particular issues of great strategic importance: enrollment levels, faculty renewal, and community outreach. He asked the committees to come back to him with ideas for change. By first trying to discern the hidden creases of his client—the faculty—Balkcom has set the stage for long-term change at St. John's that will come from within and have the support of its major constituencies.

"Mary, I'm tired of being advised. Get me someone I can boss around."

Numerous frameworks have been devised to categorize people's communications styles and personality types, and if this subject interests you, I'd suggest you explore two in particular. The first, developed by Gary Williams and Robert Miller of "Strategic Selling" fame, is based on a large study of how executives make decisions. Their results have been published in an article entitled "Change the Way You Persuade."[3] The second framework, developed many years ago by David Merrill and popularized by Robert and Dorothy Grover Bolton,[4] is based on a person's degree of assertiveness and emotional control ("responsiveness"). These approaches and others can be useful, but the difficulty I have with them is that it's hard to determine which category a client fits into. How do you know with any certainty, for example, whether a client is an "analytical" or an "expressive" (from the Bolton book)? You can develop a skill for making such distinctions, but it takes a serious investment of time.

An easier and quite powerful framework can be built around *demographics*. One advantage of using generational groups to understand clients' motivations is that you can tell immediately who belongs in which category. I conduct frequent workshops with my clients, and I was recently struck by the different habits that they have when it comes to scheduling and implementing these sessions. One, who is in his late fifties, likes to carefully plot out our schedule of meetings for months to come. He also tends to limit the participants to those who are directly involved in the issue at hand or who have a "need to know." Another client, who is in her forties, also likes to plan in advance, and she takes a slightly broader but very hierarchical view of who should come to the workshops—it's very much based on titles. Often, she wants to use a weekend to limit the number of workdays consumed. A third client is in his early thirties, and he wouldn't think of scheduling a workshop on the weekend—or on any other day when the meeting might interfere with family or personal issues. He likes to invite just about everyone and his dog to our offsites—"better to be inclusive than exclusive," he tells me; and sometimes we schedule them at the very last minute.

Sound familiar? These styles are representative of the three major demographic groups that we are now dealing with in the workplace. Each has very different goals, attitudes, and habits:

- *Traditionalists,* born before 1945 (sometimes called veterans).
- *Baby Boomers,* born between 1945 and 1964.
- *Generation Xers,* born between 1964 and 1980.

There is a fourth group, called by various names including Generation Y, the Echo Boom, and Millennials. Since they are just entering the workforce, however, we know less about how they will behave inside organizations. In terms of size, they are as numerous as the Baby Boomers, who number 79 million.

These three major generations can be further characterized:

- *Traditionalists* were born during the Depression or World War II. They are driven by loyalty and accustomed to a traditional command-and-control, hierarchical management style. They want to leave a legacy and are motivated to work for the satisfaction of a job well done. Job security is important. They can be paternalistic, and they don't believe in freely sharing information—it's on a need-to-know basis.[5]
- *Baby Boomers* are highly competitive—after all, they grew up competing with 79 million others for the best schools and jobs. For Boomers, who are mostly in their forties and early fifties, work is self-fulfillment. They are the 1960s generation at work, and they still want to shake things up and fix them. They aren't so concerned with leaving a "legacy," but they do want to have standout careers. They are motivated by money, titles, recognition, and the opportunity for self-fulfillment. Making the boss look good is important, since by doing so they enhance their own careers.

■ If Baby Boomers want an outstanding career, *Generation Xers* want a portable career—they have experienced corporate disloyalty and the erosion of trust firsthand, and their focus is more on developing their own skills than being loyal to an organization. If traditionalists are motivated by job satisfaction and leaving a legacy, and Baby Boomers value money and titles, Gen Xers want freedom. Studies consistently show that many Gen Xers will trade off money and promotions for the freedom to pursue their own interests and spend time with their families. Whereas traditionalists believe fervently in our traditional institutions, and Boomers want to change those institutions, Gen Xers are just plain skeptical—they've been burned too many times before. Boomers live to work, whereas Gen Xers work to live.

As you can see, there are some fundamental differences in the motivations and beliefs of these different generational groups. Each, in short, has its own set of "invisible creases." If you can identify them, you'll do a much better job at communicating, persuading, and managing the overall relationship.

You need to think about how to manage each of these relationships somewhat differently. Traditionalists, for example, won't be very interested in your feedback about them as managers—for someone of that generation, no news is good news when it comes to performance feedback, and getting this from an outsider would seem inappropriate. A Baby Boomer, in contrast, might relish sitting down with you and getting your views, backed up with supporting examples, particularly if your advice is going to help him better manage his career. A Gen Xer, on the other hand, would be open to frequent feedback during your time working together—she wouldn't want to wait until six months or a year had passed.

I've summarized some of approaches you might try as you manage relationships with—and try to influence—clients who belong to these three different generational groups:

Influencing Clients from Different Generations

Traditionalists (pre-1945)

- Stress how your work together will help leave a legacy.
- Ensure project goals clearly align with institutional goals.
- Carefully respect your client's guidance about who should be involved and informed.
- Emphasize the need to do the job right.

Baby Boomers (1945-1963)

- Stress the opportunity to shake things up and really fix them.
- Show how working with you can enhance their career.
- Always help your clients look good in front of their boss or senior management—respect their position in the hierarchy.
- Occasionally be prepared to provide career guidance and advice.

Generation Xers (1964-1980)

- Stress how your work together will help improve and expand your client's professional competencies and skills.
- Be highly respectful of personal time and space.
- Strive to inject fun into the relationship and project-related activities.
- Don't be put-off by skepticism—learn to overcome it by delivering the goods and showing flexibility.

Some clients will be at the cusp of one of these generational groups, with one foot in the Baby Boomer camp, for example, and another in the Generation X grouping. These individuals may, in fact, behave in ways that reflect the generations they straddle, and you need to take this into account.

Remember that this typology, like others, should be used directionally. We all know that individual behavior can often go against the norm, and we should never blindly typecast or stereotype clients. Furthermore, we need to know *ourselves*. Just as we have biases and attitudes that spring from being a man or a woman, a person of color or a WASP, so we have them based on the generation we grew up in.

It can be helpful to try to categorize your client in terms of beliefs and motivations, but equally important is careful questioning. Just as the Zen student at the beginning of this chapter had to study the boulders his teacher asked him to move, you need to do a thorough job of assessing at the outset where your clients want to go. If you don't understand the direction in which they are inclined to roll, you'll never be able to take them in the direction that *you* feel they should go.

PART ONE SUMMARY

Are You Breaking Through as an Expert?

✔ Are you focused on the three foundations of client loyalty: Adding value, developing a trusted personal relationship, and going the extra mile?

✔ If asked, would your clients be able to describe something *distinguishing* that you've done for or with them?

✔ Do you put nearly as much effort into building personal trust as you do on the technical aspects of your client engagements?

✔ Do you think of yourself as an expert for hire or as a client advisor who has both a core specialty *and* a broad knowledge of related disciplines and your clients' environment?

✔ When developing new relationships, do you seek to find commonalities, build familiarity, demonstrate openness, bring forth positive associations, praise what's positive, and cultivate rapport in face-to-face meetings?

✔ Do you directly attack clients' positions, or do you use indirect methods and humor to raise objections? Do you look for your clients' "hidden creases"—the directions they already want to go in—and use these to begin the process of influencing them?

✔ Do you focus only on the specific outcomes defined in your contractual arrangements with clients, or more broadly on improving your clients' condition in any way possible?

✔ Do you find your clients consistently keeping you at arm's length, like a supplier, or slowly bringing you into their confidences and discussing their broader issues with you?

✔ Is price becoming less important in discussions with your repeat clients?

PART TWO

MOVING INTO THE INNER CIRCLE

11

I Love My Guru . . . and Other Client Pitfalls

I'm often asked the question, "How do I handle a client who is obsessed with the latest buzz words and fascinated with gurus? I'm doing great work, but it comes across as boring compared to my competitor's flash and sizzle." Indeed, some clients love the self-proclaimed gurus who spout recycled clichés or proffer just plain bad—but sassy—advice.

Big-picture thinking, which is one of the core attributes of great advisors, is often the playground of these gurus. I've come to realize that some clients, unfortunately, don't care if an idea is right or wrong as long as it seems sufficiently bold and counter-intuitive. Let me give you an example.

A few years ago, I sat with a group of senior executives from a mid-sized company in the northeast. This was our first meeting, and they were interested in having me help them develop a turn-around strategy for the company. Also at the meeting was a well-known academic, a guru of sorts in the client's industry. The meeting was going well, and I was rather pleased with how I had conducted myself: I had listened carefully, uncovered the client's key issues, and established my credibility as an experienced strategy advisor. Right before the coffee break, I succinctly summed up the client's situation. Despite my thorough and professional approach, at the break I found myself alone, staring into my coffee. All six executives had rushed to the other end of the conference room to speak with the guru, surrounding him like fans pressing toward their favorite rock star.

What was the source of his magnetism? After my own textbook handling of the first half of the meeting and a pithy summary, he interjected and said to the group, "By the way, you need to confront the fact that the Internet is going to collapse by the end of the year. And, of course, the geo-political leaning of Russia's new leadership means that you'll have to completely rethink your Asia strategy." Just like that! Was the physical Internet actually in danger of collapsing in the next eight months? Impossible, I thought—but then again, maybe this guy knew something I didn't.

"We've got to talk," one executive shouted at the guru as I poured myself another desultory cup of coffee.

"I need to discuss the Internet with you—do you have some time later today?" asked a second.

"How can we prepare ourselves?" shouted a third client.

"I just love exchanging ideas like this," exulted yet another.

In the end, I did get the assignment—but just barely. I resolved afterwards, however, to stay away from clients who are fascinated with the "flavor-of-the-month" management approach and to focus instead on ones who appreciate insight, wisdom, and judgment grounded in solid experience.

I should add on the positive side that this experience did teach me a lesson: Clients value boldness over blandness. Does this mean you should say outrageous things to get their attention? Of course not. But I've observed a great many well-known client advisors over the years, and most of them are willing to go out on a limb, to be controversial, and to reach reasonable conclusions based on partial data. When Citibank hired strategy authority and author

I love my guru!

C. K. Prahalad as a consultant, he told them that they ought to set as a strategic goal the acquisition of one billion customers. Ridiculous, some said—at the time Citibank had only about 30 million customer relationships. In fact, such bold advice can put clients on a razor's edge—will you send them off the deep end in pursuit of something unattainable or push them to new heights? Sometimes, these big, bad ideas can help invigorate a client's own thought process, sharpening the debate.

I lived and worked in Italy for four years, and I've always remembered a delightful Italian expression often used as a commentary on interpersonal dilemmas: *"Si vede il buon giorno dalla mattina"*—"You can tell a good day from the morning." Professionals that I work with often come to me with convoluted tales about their client from hell—but usually it's an inferno they could have anticipated had they been more observant. You can often discern right from the start that you're never going to have a good relationship with a client.

Here are some warning signs to watch out for:

- Your client immediately tries to micromanage and control every facet of the relationship, rewriting your proposals, report outlines, and so on.
- Flashy appearances and public persona seem to be more important to your client than substance.
- Your client is hostile, angry, mean, or just not terribly nice. Maybe he's having a bad day; more likely, that's just his character.
- Even though others in the organization need to participate in or approve the work you're proposing, your client refuses to recognize this broader process and wants to keep you in a little box for herself.
- You discover a history of failed or conflicted relationships with previous outside professionals.
- Your client is inherently distrustful and insists on checking up on your every move.
- Your client demands disproportionate investment—in other words, he wants you to do a lot of upfront, unpaid work without any commitment or investment on his part.

Back to the question: How do you handle a client who loves his guru? You have a simple choice, really: If you're very patient and tolerant—and just can't afford to turn down the business—take the time to educate your client about the solid, day-in and day-out value you provide; otherwise, leave him to his impresarios with their "leading-edge" concepts, and move on.

Remember, carefully check the weather during your initial meetings with a client—it may save you from getting rained on later in the day.

12 | The Relationship Masters

Imagine an organization whose employees are so highly educated, versatile, and motivated that they can take on any job, anywhere in the world, and perform at the highest levels. Without visiting corporate headquarters for years at a time, employees still maintain a laser-sharp focus on their corporate mission. Imagine that these same employees are able to develop long-term advisory relationships with other professionals, business leaders, and leading politicians wherever they go, wielding an influence completely disproportionate to their relatively small numbers. An enviable set of capabilities—perhaps we're talking about General Electric or Microsoft?

No, I'm referring to the Jesuits, the Catholic order founded in 1540 by Iñigo de Oñaz y Loyola. Regardless of your religious persuasions, the Jesuits represent a fascinating case study on how to build relationship capital and become an influential advisor.

If you had been a parent to the teenage Loyola, you would have torn your hair out and despaired for his future. A Basque born in 1491, Loyola was an absolute hellion as a young man. He had a terrible character, and after a failed career as a royal pageboy and knight, he was arrested for what a judge called "atrocious crimes."

A contemporary police report described him as "cunning, violent, and vindictive." He served time in jail, and later suffered a terrible cannonball wound to his left leg, which crippled him.

Like Paul on the road to Damascus, Loyola experienced his own profound religious conversion and spent many years in quiet meditation and spiritual reflection. With the blessing of Pope Paul III, he founded the Society of Jesus with a clear, higher purpose: *ad majorem dei gloriam*—for the greater glory of God. Loyola's original concept was for a cadre of *deep generalists* who would promulgate the word of God in any place and at any time. Whereas other Catholic orders such as the Franciscans, Dominicans, and Benedictines were specialized and had a particular focus, the Jesuits would be broad-based, "polyvalent" problem-solvers who would enter many different professions. In his book, *The Jesuits,* Malachi Martin writes, "They would have to be trained not for one task, but for hundreds . . . a fast-moving strategy would be their success. Their 'specialty,' in other words, would be the ability to tackle any job expertly."[1] Jesuit priests became—depending on the requirements of their particular missions—teachers, philosophers, entomologists, paleontologists, chemists, lawyers, or any one of dozens of other professionals.

The cornerstone of the Jesuit approach was a deep, broad education. To turn out his *deep generalists,* Loyola insisted on an extraordinarily long and rigorous schooling for his priests. Young Jesuit trainees were called *scholastics* because they had to study various "schools" of knowledge: humanities, philosophy, theology, science, and so on. At his death in 1556, Loyola had founded no fewer than 35 colleges in a dozen countries. Today, Jesuit-founded universities and schools educate hundreds of thousands of students around the world.

In addition to his concept of the broadly educated problem-solver, Loyola instilled in his organization several other characteristics and practices that helped his priests become influential advisors to businessmen and politicians around the world. Both individual professionals and organizations that aspire to build their relationship capital can learn from these:

- *A higher sense of purpose.* Through their religious and spiritual training, the Jesuits were imbued with a strong sense of purpose: to peacefully spread the word of God. Having a clear mission gave the Jesuits great *conviction* in all of their dealings with other people—a hallmark of successful client advisors. Remember that experts for hire have conviction based on a belief that their information is accurate; advisors have a deeper-seated conviction based on their personal values and sense of mission.

- *Institutionalized mentoring.* Loyola institutionalized a process called the "account of conscience," whereby more seasoned Jesuits would meet regularly with less experienced ones to discuss the latter's strengths, weaknesses, hopes, fears, aspirations, and religious practice. This mentoring ensured a thoughtful and purposeful development of each young Jesuit's career, as well as a transfer of knowledge and experience from one generation to the next.

- *Independence.* The Jesuits were created as a distinct and separate organization that reported directly to the Pope. Wherever they operated around the world, they were independent of the main Catholic hierarchy. Jesuits were free, in other words, to pursue their mission without getting embroiled in or stymied by the vast church bureaucracy. Another factor that contributed to the Jesuits' independence: For many centuries they were banned from acting as principles in any type of business, a policy that had the effect of lending great credibility and objectivity to the advice they gave to their business and political contacts. This independence helped the Jesuits form myriad relationships that would have been impossible to develop if they had had particular political leanings or were engaged in conflicting business interests.

- *An understanding of the mind and soul of their converts.* Despite their fierce allegiance to the Pope and Catholic doctrine, the Jesuits showed enormous empathy in trying to win converts. In eighteenth-century China, the Jesuits were the only religious order that *ever* succeeded at converting great numbers of the Chinese to Christianity. Other missionaries had prohibited the dearly held Chinese ceremonies honoring the Emperor, Confucius, and one's ancestors. As a result, they failed miserably in their efforts to proselytize. Through detailed analysis of Chinese writings and practices, the Jesuits demonstrated to the Pope that these rituals did not venerate Confucius or the Emperor as divinities, and that furthermore, the Chinese people would never accept Christianity if these rites were banned. Only if the church accepted these local customs, they argued, would the locals in turn accept Christianity.

Wherever they were posted in the world, Jesuit priests tried to absorb local customs and language. Pedro Arrupe, for example, who headed the Jesuits during the last century, lived in Japan for many years and became a complete Japanophile during his stay. He spoke perfect Japanese, and even used to pray sitting on a cushion in the Zen meditation position.

Baltasar Gracián also typified the success achieved by the many Jesuits who benefited from this system of personal development and professional practice. A sixteenth-century Jesuit priest and author who advised many influential Spaniards, Gracián was befriended by a wealthy nobleman named Vicencio Juan de Lastanosa. De Lastanosa had a huge library in his baronial mansion and granted Gracián full access to it. Delighted with the company of such a highly educated, learned individual (a rarity in those days), de Lastanosa later paid for the publication of several of Gracián's books. One of them, *The Art of Worldly Wisdom,* continues to be widely sold today. De Lastanosa was a true *catalyst* for Gracián, helping him to reach and influence many other important Spaniards. Gracián, in turn, served as a counselor—a mentor—to the younger Lastanosa, advising him on everything from the expansion of his library to his family relationships.

As a result, of these practices, many leaders throughout history have turned to individual Jesuits for counsel and advice, valuing their enormous breadth of learning, independence, and objectivity (in sec-ular affairs, at least), and impeccable integrity. What accrued to the Jesuits was an abundance of relationship capital—a wide circle of accomplished companions, wealthy political and business figures who acted as catalysts to further the Jesuits' mission, and an abundance of "clients" (converts, in this case) who were won by the Jesuits' abil-ity to empathize and understand their minds and souls.

13 | The Doubting Mind

"I used to work for an old-fashioned rainmaker," a client of mine once told me. "He had that 'take-no-prisoners' approach to sales and customer relationships. His motto was, 'Sometimes wrong, never in doubt.'" Never in doubt, indeed. It's one thing to have deep-seated convictions about your views, quite another to obscure the truth with overconfidence and bluster—something that clients today won't put up with.

Doubt plays an important role for client advisors who build long-term relationships. There are three types of doubt that are useful to cultivate:

1. *External doubt.* Skepticism that what your clients tell you about their problems is really true, and a willingness to challenge conventional wisdom.
2. *Internal doubt.* The ability to step back and recognize that you may be wrong.
3. *Doubt about outcomes.* The willingness to suspend judgment about what's "good" and "bad" about events whose eventual consequences we cannot, in truth, fully predict.

First, great advisors are bit skeptical about what clients tell them. They watch clients' feet, not their mouths. They are convinced by observable behavior and data, not by mere words. Client advisors, metaphorically, all come from Missouri—the "Show-Me" state.

Schroders, the global merchant banking firm, should have been so lucky. In the early 1980s, when the London financial markets were deregulated, a strict separation between investment banking (securities underwriting and issuance) and brokering (distribution and trading) took place. As these walls were removed, it was assumed that *every* merchant bank would have to rush into stockbroking in order to hold onto its market share and client base. When Schroders, one of the top three merchant banks at the time, hired James Kelly as its advisor, they expected to receive similar advice—the question was really how to implement this shift. Kelly, who had deep experience in the U.S. financial markets, thought it would be suicide for Schroders to plunge into a trading business they knew nothing about. Rejecting the accepted wisdom, he convinced Schroders to remain independent and focus on its core strengths—investment banking, mergers and acquisitions, and fund management. One by one, its competitors tried to become full-service banks, and one by one, they stumbled and were picked off by larger institutions at bargain prices. Sixteen years later, Schroders' market value had increased more than 25-fold and, at the peak of the market, it sold its highly valued investment banking business to Citigroup, where it continues to prosper (the fund management side remained independent). Kelly, who founded and was CEO of a major consulting firm, says, "You have to be skeptical when you see the herd thundering in one direction. You just have to doubt whether it makes sense for your client."

Alan Weiss, a popular author and consultant known for his contrarian views, tells a similar story: "The CEO of a division of a Fortune 500 company asked me to improve his company's sales effectiveness and closing time. When I asked him why, he said that that they had 25 percent annual 'uncontrollable' customer attrition, which necessitated increasing their acquisition efforts. When I asked him what uncontrollable attrition was, he said that some customers went out of business, were acquired by larger companies, or stopped being customers for reasons completely outside the client's control. I then pressed him to tell me how he knew this, and he explained that the sales force carefully collected and reported these statistics to him. So I set out to find out for myself, and personally interviewed a group of customers who had left for 'uncontrollable' reasons. Ninety percent had, in fact, defected due to poor service or other reasons completely *within* the control of this company. They didn't need more sales effectiveness—they needed to address a host of other issues such as quality and service. You can't always accept clients' basic premises."

How often have you heard the following assertions?

- "We have the best quality in the business."
- "Our management team is second to none."
- "We have the lowest employee attrition in our industry."
- "Our competitor's products use inferior/outdated/incompatible technology."
- "We've already implemented that" [whatever it is you're suggesting to them].
- "Our brand is one of our most valuable assets."
- "I manage my own investments and do much better than the pros."

As an advisor, you should politely question and challenge statements like these. Ask for evidence that they are true. Through direct inquiry, find out for yourself. Your clients will, ultimately, thank you.

The flip side of doubting your client's assertions or rejecting accepted wisdom is questioning your own premises. One of the traps that experts fall into is a blind belief in their infallible expertise. Many governmental and corporate blunders—for example, the Iran-Contra scandal of the 1980s and the dot-com meltdown of the late 1990s, just to cite some contemporary examples—can be traced to this hubris.

My brother, a prominent surgeon, told me about a medical case that illustrates the dangers of a lack of doubt: "A patient at my hospital," he explained, "had suffered a brain injury, and it was determined that he was essentially 'brain dead'—according to his doctors, there was no hope whatsoever of recovery. He would never regain consciousness. The family, ever hopeful, refused to allow life support to be removed. For months, the man lay in a vegetative coma. One day, a nurse was brushing his teeth, and he suddenly blurted out, 'Leave me alone!' He did something that the medical experts considered an impossibility."

I recall a client in Italy who asked a major consulting firm to evaluate a proposal to open several bank branches in Milan. The firm had extensive experience in the banking industry and had developed a sophisticated model for determining branch profitability. The model, in essence, showed that a bank could become profitable by clustering its branches in one geographic location rather than dispersing them. They told my client, in no uncertain terms, that to open just a few branches in the north of Italy would be a disaster. Instead, they said, he should concentrate new branches near his existing ones in central Italy. Against the consultants' advice, my client opened the Milan branches, and they were a huge success. I won't go into all the reasons why they worked out so well—but the consultants had applied a business model that had worked in many other countries, notably the United States, without understanding this client's particular context and business environment. They refused to entertain any doubts about their stock advice. As a result, they left behind one very dissatisfied client.

The third type of doubt you need to exercise is about *outcomes*. In the West, we are very certain that some things are good for us and others are bad. A competitor comes out with a similar product or service to one that we offer—terrible! We are audited by the IRS— horrendous! Someone threatens to sue us—heinous! At other times, we are sure some events are good. We get offered a promotion, for example, or better yet, win the lottery. What great fortune, everyone says.

Zen philosophy, in contrast, espouses a neutral attitude toward the world and the events of life. It encourages us to doubt our pre-conceived notions about events being either favorable or unfavor-able. Apparent disasters may be blessings in disguise, just as much as windfall events can bring trouble and sadness. You've won the lot-tery? You should read the studies that have been done of lottery winners—for many of them, winning the lottery ruined their lives! On the flip side, when a competing product hits the market, why are we so sure that's a bad thing? Perhaps the new product will stimulate the market and renew demand for our own product; or the competition will spur our organization toward greater innova-tion, resulting in increased profits down the road. After Bernie Marcus was *fired* from Kmart, he promptly went out and cofounded Home Depot—he's now a billionaire.

This principle is beautifully illustrated in W. Somerset Maugham's short story "The Verger," in which a man named Albert has been the verger (a lay caretaker) at a small church for 16 years. One day a new vicar arrives at the church, and, discovering that Albert cannot read or write, fires him. Feeling depressed and desti-tute as he walks along the street near the church, Albert notices that there are no shops nearby, and decides to start a small kiosk selling tobacco and candy. He proves to be quite adept at business, and in a short time ends up owning a whole chain of kiosks and shops. Years later, Albert has become a very wealthy man. One day he goes to the local bank to make a large deposit and asks the bank manager for as-sistance, casually explaining that he cannot read or write. Hearing his story, the manager exclaims in astonishment, "Good God, man! What would you be now if you had been able to?"

"I can tell you that, sir," replies Albert. "I'd be verger of St. Peter's, Neville Square."[1]

So don't be so sure that an outcome is good or bad for your client—or for yourself. Remember the old Zen saying, "Small doubt, small enlightenment; great doubt, great enlightenment."[2] Things may not turn out to be as bad—or as good—as you think they will. The next time a client turns you down, don't wring your hands and mope around the house; it's not the end of the world, and another door may open for you where you least expect it. Correspondingly, when you win a big assignment or your client scores a victory, celebrate but don't think all your problems are over—you and I both know they aren't!

14 | The Deep Generalist and the Branded Expert

Few of us could forget the trial of O. J. Simpson in 1996, and the unprecedented media frenzy that surrounded it. It was a drama that included a remarkable cast of legal talent and more than a few larger-than-life personalities, including the flamboyant Johnny Cochran, the notorious F. Lee Bailey, and Harvard Law School professor Alan Dershowitz, famed for his defense of Claus von Bulow, Michael Milken, and Mike Tyson. Rounding out the defense team, Barry Scheck confounded the prosecution with his extraordinary grasp of the esoteric science of DNA analysis.

So how does the O. J. trial relate to making rain for your clients? It's actually very relevant. Cochran, Bailey, and Dershowitz were the *deep generalists* on the case, with Dershowitz being an especially good example. A fierce client advocate, he is deeply grounded in several legal specialties, but at the same time has an extremely broad understanding of the law. He has written over a dozen books, covering topics as diverse as the U.S. Constitution, the criminal justice system, and politics and the law. He is active in a variety of nonprofit causes. He reads widely and is, well, kind of a Renaissance man. A popular professor of law, he has successfully taken on a diversity of cases.

In contrast, Barry Scheck, at least in the eye of the public, is a *branded expert.* He has carved out a very specific niche in forensic DNA analysis. The media seek him out for comment and "expert" analysis on this specific topic. Dershowitz and Scheck illustrate two career paths—or at least two sides of our career development—for professionals of all types: the *deep generalist* and the *branded expert.*

In Chapter 2, I said that the vast majority of professionals who develop broad-based, long-term client relationships are *deep generalists.* They have great depth of knowledge in one or two core specialties, and a breadth of knowledge about their clients' organization, industry, and environment. They read widely, and part of their stock-and-trade is to bring big-picture thinking to their clients. They move beyond just providing data and information— something that ordinary experts can do—to become educators and navigators to their clients. Deep generalists tend to have a small- to medium-size group of clients whom they serve as trusted advisors.

Whereas the deep generalist builds a broad base of knowledge and gets closer to clients, a *branded expert* goes deeper into a specific expertise. These experts deliberately and systematically use a variety of distribution channels and media to disseminate and publicize their ideas and expertise. They publish articles and books; "productize" their intellectual capital in the form of seminars, workshops, and curricula; exploit broadcast media; create tapes and videos; leverage the Internet; and develop expert software to allow access to their ideas without having to appear in person.

In the field of management Ken Blanchard of *One Minute Manager* fame and the Stern Stewart consulting firm are both good examples of branded experts. On the one hand, Blanchard publishes prolifically on employee motivation and customer loyalty. His consulting and training company disseminates his ideas through workshops, tapes, and videos. Stern Stewart, on the other hand, specializes in consulting on economic value added (EVA). Its founders took some basic financial theories about the relationship between cost of capital and return on capital, and packaged them into the EVA concept. The Stern Stewart consulting firm sells software to help companies implement and manage shareholder value concepts, but its consulting platform is narrow rather than deep—in contrast, say, to McKinsey, which represents the deep generalist strategy.

Branded experts are different from "plain-vanilla" experts or experts for hire, as I call them. The services of experts for hire can be traded as if they were commodities. Branded experts, in contrast, are *über-experts* who gain extensive notoriety and who aggressively employ a variety of strategies to get their ideas out to as many potential clients as possible.

In summary, deep generalists develop a selected group of broad-based, advisory client relationships, whereas branded experts have a large number of narrow relationships and are more transactionally focused. Deep generalists go deeper into their client relationships; branded experts focus on increased mastery of their specialized expertise.

Some of you are no doubt asking, "Can't you be both a deep generalist and a branded expert? Don't deep generalists have to follow many of the same media- and publishing-focused strategies that characterize branded experts?"

Yes, many deep generalists also publish, give workshops, use the Internet, and become well known for a specific expertise. In fact, some have multiple brands that appeal to different client bases.

Deep generalists and branded experts often borrow from each other's playbooks, and some may indeed maintain dual identities. Among a small group of clients, I am known as a generalist strategy advisor, a trusted advisor with a small number of deep, long-term client relationships. In broader circles, I'm the "client relationship expert," a branded expert who does speeches, workshops, and consulting on keeping clients and customers for the long term.

There is a subtle tension between these two strategies, however, because they represent different business models with different key success factors. In practice, I could spend 100 percent of my time on being the branded expert, building more products and even software around client relationship development, creating training companies, and so on. But then I wouldn't have any time to provide in-depth advice to clients and cultivate long-term relationships with them, something that I enjoy immensely.

Ultimately, the distinction between a deep generalist and a branded expert is useful for two reasons: First, it highlights important sides of any advisor's persona that require development; and second, it calls attention to a natural tension and a set of choices that need to be consciously balanced.

Within large professional service firms, this dichotomy has some very practical implications. Among your staff, what mix of deep generalists and branded experts do you want, and how do you make room for both types of professionals? How you respond to these questions depends on your strategy: Relationship-oriented firms such as bankers Goldman Sachs and consultants McKinsey & Company tend to cultivate many deep generalists within their ranks; specialist firms such as consultants Stern Stewart or boutique law firms have a preponderance of branded experts. You need career tracks for both types of professionals, with distinct approaches to training and development, different compensation metrics, and appropriate mentoring. In working with clients, there is a delicate art to putting teams together with just the right mix of generalist versus specialist skills.

The different tactics required to pursue this balance are summarized in the following figure:

Deep Generalists versus Branded Experts

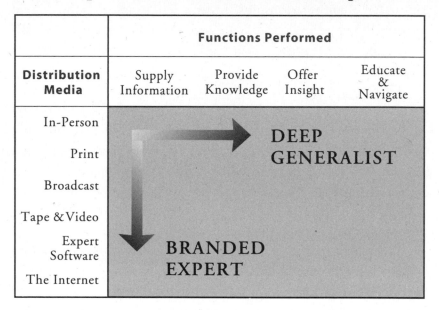

Distribution Media	Functions Performed			
	Supply Information	Provide Knowledge	Offer Insight	Educate & Navigate
In-Person				
Print			DEEP GENERALIST	
Broadcast				
Tape & Video				
Expert Software	BRANDED EXPERT			
The Internet				

Which strategy, or mix of strategies, is right for you? It depends on several factors. Are you a solo practitioner, or do you work within a large firm? If you work on your own, you're going to have to develop at least *some* of the deep generalist capabilities that I've described; otherwise, your ability to market yourself and acquire new clients will be handicapped. Inside a large firm it may be possible to carve out a purely specialist niche, leaving client acquisition and management to others.

By dint of personality, skills, and the activities you enjoy, are you oriented toward great depth in one subject matter, or do you have broader interests you want to pursue? Do you relish developing one or two ideas and then getting them across to dozens or hundreds of clients around the country, or do you prefer to dig in with a few clients and really get to know their people and their organizations?

One thing is for sure: You don't want to be stuck in the old-fashioned expert-for-hire role, which in today's markets is tantamount to being a vendor—a commodity. You've got to distinguish yourself, which you can do by developing close, broad-based client relationships where you play the role of navigator and educator, or by creating a branded persona around a specific expertise. Some professionals will be able to combine elements of both of these. Whatever path you choose, do it consciously and deliberately, and make sure that it plays to *your own* particular strengths.

15 | How to Identify Client Needs

"I've met several times with the CEO," I told my colleagues, "and his need is pretty clear: His company is faltering abroad, and he wants to develop a new international strategy to help jump-start growth outside the United States." At the time, I was a senior partner with a large international consulting firm. The occasion was an account development session to brainstorm a new proposal for a prospective client. I had carefully reviewed all of the background information on the company and summarized for the assembled group how I thought we could help.

In the back of the room, someone piped up, "This company doesn't just need an international strategy—it needs to completely transform its business."

"That may be," I replied, "but I think right now the international piece is what the CEO is focused on." A chorus of voices drowned me out, insisting that I had misread the situation and that what the client really needed was a wholesale overhaul of its organization, including its operations, marketing, and sales.

"This company is a prime candidate for our business transformation services," one of my colleagues informed me, even as I kept resisting.

102

"They need to take a fresh look at the U.S. market as well," said another.

"Get with the program!" urged a third.

Frustrated, I ended the session and thanked everyone for contributing. A few months later, I left the firm to start my own independent consulting practice.

This anecdote illustrates a major pitfall of trying to identify client needs: The inability to separate out what *you* think the client needs—or what you need personally—from what the *client really* needs. All too often, we look at our clients' situation through the lens of our own service offerings and our own desire for a sale, and fail to understand the best way to help them.

Identifying how you can help your clients isn't always easy. Sometimes clients themselves don't know what they want or need. Here are seven strategies that can help you get in touch with your clients' needs.

1. Create a Client Panel

Every year in March, Environmental Resources Management (ERM), a large environmental services consulting firm, brings its senior management and about 35 top clients to a summit meeting in Phoenix, Arizona. Many companies hold meetings like this, but they tend to be "schmoozfests" with lots of golf and alcohol and a few morning seminars where subject matter experts hold forth for an hour or two. ERM takes a very different approach: Its senior executives conduct workshops to explore the most important and problematic issues that its client executives face, as defined by the executives themselves. These executives share experiences in an open atmosphere, and ERM opens a valuable window onto the daily challenges facing its clients, who in turn benefit from valuable, peer-to-peer exchanges.

"But doesn't it seem like you're pumping them for their issues just to go back later and try to sell them on something?" I asked an ERM board member who participates in these sessions.

"It works precisely because we *don't* do that," he replied. "We don't go back a month later and try to sell them on a solution to an issue they raised and that, by itself, reinforces trust. Just by creating these forums, we're adding value in ways that our competitors can't and don't. The experience enhances our relationship with the executives, giving us insight into their issues; thus, we're able to better evolve our own service offerings."

Some firms create a small client panel that has a fixed number (10 or 15) of client executives who meet once or twice a year to provide advice on overall strategy and service offering development. Others, such as ERM, invite to an annual event a large group of clients, whose composition changes slightly from year to year.

2. Conduct Industry Research and Analysis

This is a time-honored approach to uncovering potential client needs, and it can also garner valuable publicity. I recall vividly a study done some years ago by the MAC Group, a Boston-based strategy consulting boutique where I began my own consulting career and that later became part of Cap Gemini. The MAC Group had analyzed the financial performance of hundreds of publicly held banks and sorted them into four groups with catchy names. The "sharks," whose returns well exceeded their cost of equity, were poised to eat the "minnows," whose profitability was weak. The study attracted enormous media attention and stimulated a lot of meetings with potential clients to talk about their position in the industry and whether they were doing enough to bolster their financial returns. Sometimes, simple frameworks that you synthesize from industry research (remember Boston Consulting Group's "Growth-Share Matrix"?) can become powerful tools to get clients to open up and discuss their issues.

Despite the effectiveness of this type of research, it is typically the domain of high-end consulting firms. Other professional service firms—for example, in law, public relations, and accounting–do far less of it, which is a mistake. As these markets become increasingly competitive, the firms that thrive will be the ones that are very skilled at knowledge creation.

3. Invest Extra Time to Get to Know Your Client

During the normal course of your work with clients, you'll have the opportunity for exposure to their organization and operations. Are you prepared to invest the extra time required to truly get to know them? If you and your firm are busy, this can be hard to do—your time is probably already tightly allocated among competing demands. But going the extra mile—which is part of the loyalty equation—can yield you valuable insights that you won't pick up any other way. This means offering to attend meetings that you haven't necessarily been invited to, working hard to expand your network of relationships within your client's organization, and investing in deep client learning.

My father, a retired psychiatrist who chaired the department of child psychiatry at Dartmouth Medical School, used to have a packed schedule of patients nearly every day. A highly successful therapist, he routinely did something very unusual that set him apart from all of his peers: Early in his relationship with each patient, he visited the patient in his home or family environment. He describes his unique approach this way:

> I almost got kicked out of the psychoanalytic society for doing home visits. They had this crazy notion that you had to be unseen and ambiguous—a nonperson—in your treatment of patients. I wanted to see what was going on in patients' homes, however. I learned a tremendous amount that helped me be a better therapist. When you walk into the house of a patient and you almost fall through a hole in the hallway floorboards that's been there for two years, what does it say? Or you get there, and an enormous German Shepard is lunging at the screen door and the patient tells you, "Oh, we forgot to tell you about the dog"—what does it say about their relationship to you? I would

ask for a tour of the house, which might be a disaster . . . or so compulsively clean you could eat off the floor. You'd see how kids kept their rooms, what they put on the walls. For five minutes they would act like they do in therapy, but after that they would revert to their real selves and lapse into their normal relationships—the children would be eating standing up, the husband and wife would stop talking to each other and so on.

"Why don't all therapists do this?" I asked him. You can probably anticipate his answer:

A home visit could take three or four hours. Therapists don't know *how* to bill for it or *if* they can bill for this kind of time. Furthermore, from a personal point of view, visiting a patient outside your office makes you vulnerable. What does it say if you drive up in a BMW or in an old wreck? What if you're a few minutes late? How will you react to an embarrassing situation?

The dynamics my father describes closely resemble those of client relationships in a business setting. The insights you gain from taking the time to make, metaphorically, a "home visit" to your client's world, the difficulty of billing for the time you spend, the personal vulnerability you feel—most of us have experienced these with our clients.

4. Talk to Your Client's Customers

Talking to your client's customers can yield valuable insights into service requirements, new product opportunities, and competitive trends. I've seen firms do this in the proposal stage, subsequently embedding valuable perspectives about the client's strengths and weaknesses in the final proposal, as well as doing it during a paid project. Some former colleagues of mine wrote an excellent article on this subject, "Spend a Day in the Life of Your Customer," which was published in the *Harvard Business Review*.[1] The concept is that by understanding the needs and everyday business problems of your clients' customers, you will have a better idea of what you can do for your client.

5. Ask

Asking your clients directly about their needs is tricky, for several reasons. They may not actually be aware of what they really need, or they simply may not open up to you. They may also omit something because they don't perceive you as a resource to deal with it. This doesn't mean you shouldn't try, however. Generally, I find indirect questions work better than direct ones. Here are some suggested phrasings:

- "What's keeping you awake at night?"
- "When you're stuck in traffic, and you're thinking about the business, what runs through your head?"
- "You've told me about your strategy and goals. Are there any soft spots you're concerned about? Where's the greatest risk of failure or of falling short?"
- "If you successfully achieve these goals, what will be different or better? How will things be different for the average employee or customer a year from now?"

Most clients are occasionally kept awake at night by a concern or worry. One client, however, once replied to me, "Nothing keeps me up—I sleep like a baby every night." It turned out he was an individual fundamentally motivated to capture the next opportunity rather than solve problems.

To have the right to ask these types of questions, you need to establish some credibility with the client. Some of the techniques for doing this are described in Chapters 4 and 25.

Another good technique to draw a client out is to use comparative frameworks, which will vary depending on your profession or industry. Here are some examples:

- "Some companies take a market-based approach to compensation, whereas others are driven by internal equity. Still others develop a mix of the two criteria. Where do you fall on this spectrum?"
- "As you move forward with this program, which is your greatest concern—speed, quality, or cost?"
- "Some of our clients are investing in global branding; others are creating a family of distinct brands. How would you characterize your approach?"
- "Where would you put yourself on a scale between these two extremes—wanting to earn the highest possible returns on your investments or preserving your capital at all costs?"

I find that clients respond well to these conversation starters that ask them to place themselves on a continuum. They are a useful way of getting clients to talk about themselves.

6. Use Comparative Benchmarks

Using comparative and competitive benchmarks is an excellent way to stimulate your client's thinking and get him or her to talk about possible needs. It's quite powerful when you can say to a client, "Your company spends 9 percent of revenue on sales, whereas the industry average is 5 percent. What do you think accounts for the difference?" You might get a number of responses to this question, including: "We serve more small- and mid-size customers than our competitors, and that drives our cost of sales way up. We really would like to migrate upward, but right now I don't think we have the correct product suite," or, "We have high-quality individuals on our salesforce, but they lack selling skills and product knowledge."

In a different realm, I know a litigation attorney who has at his fingertips a variety of statistics on the success rates of different types of litigation in various courts. He uses these very effectively with clients, comparing their own track records to the averages, and drawing out their perception of their strengths, weaknesses, and potential future needs in regard to litigation.

7. Talk to Company Observers

There are many sources of data and perspectives on a given company that you can tap as a way of identifying client needs. If the company is publicly held, stock analysts can be an excellent source of information, and nowadays, many of their reports can be obtained at no cost from your broker or banker. Other "experts" can include suppliers, consultants who specialize in the industry, and trade association executives.

"Hello Mr. Smith. I'm the CEO of a Fortune-500 company that needs a LOT of help. Although our strategy has failed and our core processes are broken, we still have lots of cash. I'm looking for a long-term relationship, not a one-off transaction. And the only name my board gave me to call was yours."

Keep in mind that a client's need for your services will often be triggered by observable events. These include a merger or acquisition, a change in leadership, a reorganization, a new competitor, new regulations, new technology, and changes in its financial condition or stock price. You need to be constantly attuned to these internal and external events, and ready both to interpret their implications for your client and respond to clients' specific requests.

Identifying client needs is sometimes easiest, ironically, when you first begin the relationship—usually the client has carefully thought through what he wants and is actively reaching out to engage a professional to solve a particular problem. It's later on, as the relationship evolves, that it gets harder—the urgency has diminished, and the client, having tackled an important issue, may feel that things are on a more even keel. If you want to systematically tune into legitimate ways you can help improve your client's business, you need to utilize both institutional mechanisms such as client panels and industry research, and ad hoc approaches such as customer interviewing, "walking the halls," competitive benchmarking, and soliciting company observers. Behind all of these has to be the explicit willingness to invest personal time and resources in the relationship.

Think about your two or three highest potential clients. What investment are you making today to learn about their needs and build for the future?

16 | The Power of Size

Developing Large, Multi-Year Client Relationships

Mel Immergut, a masterful client advisor and the chairman of leading law firm Milbank Tweed, once described to me how he developed a major relationship:

> An attorney, who had helped my firm on a case a number of years ago, became the general counsel of a Fortune 500 corporation. I called on him several times to see if Milbank could assist his company on a particular legal issue. Unfortunately, the CEO had a strong existing relationship with several other law firms, and nothing came of the discussions. Finally, though, the general counsel saw an opening for us to help on a very narrow, targeted issue, and he managed to bring us in. The company had some investments that had not gone well, and they needed help in sorting these out. Several of our associates threw themselves into the work, devoting themselves to learning everything they could about these investments and the client's organization. A year later, the client was immensely impressed by both the quality of the work and the personal dedication they saw in our attorneys. We quickly became *the* law firm to handle all their legal work surrounding these investments.

I continued to meet regularly with the general counsel, and discovered they were trying to grapple with some sticky issues around patents and intellectual property as they bought up new companies. I talked about our very strong intellectual property practice, and he asked us to handle one specific case. I suggested we go further and hold a daylong working session, hosted by our most experienced partners, which would focus on a broad set of intellectual property issues. Their top people flew in for this session, which was highly successful, and we were soon handling a large amount of this client's intellectual property work.

In another meeting with the general counsel, I discovered they were trying to expand their business in Asia. I had one of our associates in Asia spend several weeks with the client's executives in that region, and we were able to propose several good ideas for how best to structure the new company. More work for us in Asia followed.

Based on what had now emerged as a broad-based, long-term relationship, the client asked us to do some work in a very specialized area of the law that we have never cultivated as a firm. It was tempting to use this as a platform to develop a capability, but I decided instead to recommend a small, specialist firm. Sometimes you just have to know what you're good at and not good at, and be honest with the client about your capabilities.

Immergut's success is not an accident. He and his firm:

- Carefully followed up on Immergut's relationship with the individual who later became the chief legal officer for a major corporation.
- Did an extraordinarily good job on a small, initial piece of work, and also cultivated strong personal relationships with the local client.
- Followed up regularly with senior management to assess the progress of the work.

- Constantly kept attuned to other possible areas of need.
- Invested in an expensive working session with top partners that turned a small opportunity (one piece of patent work) into another major axis of the relationship.
- Turned down an assignment where Milbank could not deliver at the top level and introduced a specialist firm that could better meet the client's needs.

Large-scale client relationships can offer huge rewards. For both firms and individual practitioners, just one large relationship can transform the practice. I recall that when I moved to London in the early 1980s to help my firm develop its international practice, there were just four of us in a small, one-room office. (The nearest bathroom was four stories above us!) Over the next two years, we developed three major, multimillion-dollar relationships—two with major banks and a third with a large U.K. industrial company—that grew our backlog from two to nearly twelve months of work. We hired several dozen highly talented consultants who were eager to join a fast-growing consulting practice, and we were able to move into a new office (it even had its own bathroom). Best of all, we did great work for these three clients and, with those references in hand, grew the business to over 100 consultants in just a few years.

Here are some of the many benefits you can accrue from these types of relationships:

- *Economies of scale.* Managing and administering a large relationship doesn't take up much more time than it does for a small one. The ratio of dollars of revenue per unit of your time is more favorable. Profit margins can also be much higher on large projects (sometimes the reverse is true, and large orders are won only on the basis of volume discounts, which reduce gross margins. Many other important benefits still apply, however).

- *Secure backlog that enables you to hire and grow.* If all you have are short assignments, it's harder to make the investments in hiring, people development, R&D, and marketing that are necessary to grow your business.
- *The opportunity to become highly knowledgeable about your client's organization and business.* A one-week project with a client or a very small order doesn't allow you to gain that much knowledge about your client. A large piece of work typically plunges you deeply into the client's company, and the intimate knowledge you develop of his needs becomes a major barrier for competing firms to overcome. You also become exposed to a variety of other potential buyers in the client's organization.
- *Valuable intellectual capital.* Large, complex client relationships such as the one described by Mel Immergut encourage a firm to develop invaluable skills and experiences dealing with difficult, sophisticated business issues.

Conversely, many small client relationships can lead to high overhead costs as a percentage of revenue, lack of a stable backlog, and work that lacks depth.

Because of these factors, many firms are careful not to take on too many small assignments unless there are clear reasons for doing so. These could include growth potential, the opportunity to learn something important or new, the opportunity to develop younger staff, and so on. When strategy consulting firm Bain & Company was expanding internationally, for example, it only opened an office in a country once it had acquired a flagship client there. This strategy resulted in a profitable set of offices right at the start. Bain's practice stands in sharp contrast to that of many other companies that have typically opened an office first—with all of its associated overhead—and then slowly tried to grow a client base.

There are also risks involved in developing large-scale clients. If an unduly high percentage of your revenue derives from one client, your business can be seriously damaged if you lose that account, something that can happen frequently in the advertising profession. Furthermore, your independence and judgment can be adversely affected by the steady stream of cash, a phenomenon symptomatic of a number of major corporate scandals in recent years (think of Enron, Sunbeam, and Waste Management). Large, long-term relationships make sense only if your client continues to benefit from your work. It will almost always end badly if you start feeding at the trough, so to speak, while the client gets diminishing returns.

In thinking about how to grow relationships, you have to consider both how you initially engage a client and what your migration strategy is afterward.

Developing Large-Scale Client Relationships

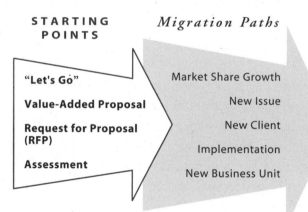

Keep in mind that average relationship size can be a key driver of your growth and profitability. Your revenues are based on the number of opportunities you see, times the percent that you win, times the average size of each engagement. If you contain your selling costs while increasing the size of your relationships, you can significantly increase both the profitability and growth of your business.

In the next chapter, I'll talk about the four starting points for a relationship. Then in Chapter 18, I'll address five strategies for growing a relationship once that relationship has begun.

17 | The Right Foot

Four Ways to Start a Relationship and Position It for the Long Term

When you begin a relationship with a new client, you want to position your firm and your work in a way that maximizes, right from the start, the long-term potential of the relationship. Even in the proposal stage, you need to differentiate yourself as someone who has great expertise but who acts like an advisor rather than an expert for hire whose proposals are indistinguishable from those of other experts.

This chapter looks at four ways a relationship can get started. I have not tried to provide a comprehensive treatment of all aspects of proposal writing or marketing to new clients; instead, for each option I've highlighted a few reminders that will help position you for success and growth.

1. Let's Go

Sometimes a client has in mind a specific assignment and, because she knows you or because you've been highly recommended to her, she may be willing to start work with only minimal documentation.

She calls you up and says, "Let's get going." This kind of eagerness usually happens with relatively small projects or orders—unless you have a long-standing relationship, it's unlikely someone is going to give you a multimillion-dollar assignment without going through a more detailed proposal process.

Here's what you need to watch out for in these cases:

- *Clear needs and objectives.* Even though you're not writing a formal proposal, you still need to clarify and articulate the client's need, what his objectives are for the work, what it is you're actually going to do, and how success is going to be measured. Without a clear articulation of these issues, you risk a fatal misunderstanding.

- *A focus on the right problem.* You need to make sure you're not underselling yourself and overlooking the client's real problem. One of the hallmarks of a client advisor—versus an expert for hire—is the willingness and vision to slow the client down and look at the bigger picture. Sometimes clients rush to start something without taking the time to think the whole project through. How does the proposed work relate to other initiatives? Does it have the full support of senior management? Are there any detractors in the organization with whom you'll have to deal? Does management have divergent perspectives on how the work should be done and the nature of the problem itself?

- *Proper positioning.* If you're starting on a small piece of work, it's especially important to position your capabilities properly with the client; otherwise, you'll be forever pigeonholed as someone who does tiny things. If I accept an assignment to do a day's worth of work analyzing a client's competitor, for example, and I haven't set the right context, I risk being labeled as "the competitive analysis guy" who does one-day projects! We naturally position people and their capabilities, and put them into a slot. Don't let your clients do this to you.

2. Value-Added Proposals

When you write a value-added proposal, you invest significant resources to understand the client, his problem, and the potential solutions. An advertising agency would put together a sample set of advertisements. A consulting firm might exhaustively analyze a client's competitive position and perhaps even interview the client's customers to shed light on the significant issues. A company selling sophisticated software might do a comprehensive needs analysis and draw up detailed implementation proposals, whereas a financial advisor will typically do an in-depth analysis of a potential client's current financial position. I know firms that will spend 10 percent to 20 percent of a contract's potential value on developing a value-added proposal—not an insignificant sum! A well-conceived value-added proposal, in short, can be instrumental in winning large contracts.

Here are some principles to follow in developing value-added proposals:

- *Maximize face-to-face meetings.* The more face-to-face meetings you have with the client prior to submitting a final proposal, the higher your likelihood of winning. If you get four meetings to your competitor's two, you have the advantage. Clients (like the rest of us) do business with people they like (see Chapter 7), and familiarity is one of the main drivers of likability. Furthermore, your sense of the client's needs and context will be sharpened by each direct encounter.
- *Be insightful.* Always provide a valuable insight, conceptual framework, or piece of information in the proposal that is fresh and new to the client. This could be a tidbit of information about a competitor that the client is unfamiliar with, or some surprising piece of customer feedback. Think of a value-added proposal, at least in part, as a report to your client describing how he can improve his business. When a client reads your proposal, he should feel that the assignment has already started and you are already adding value.

- *Show you're a peer.* Value-added proposals should read like a partnership contract, rather than a sales document prepared for a potential buyer. You need to spell out not just what you are going to do but also what the client's responsibilities are.
- *Get conceptual agreement first.* The final written proposal should ideally be no more than a record of work you have already agreed to do for the client. In other words, there is conceptual agreement on the approach and the expected results; the proposal is just a formality.[1] Naturally, if the bid is competitive, this may be harder to accomplish. Avoid shooting proposals off in the mail or through e-mail (which clients often ask us to do) without first reaching agreement. Your odds will never be great with this "light a candle and pray" approach.

3. Request for Proposal (RFP)

Everyone hates RFPs because they strip away much of your ability to add value during the proposal process and to differentiate yourself from the competition. Companies that issue RFPs typically limit access to their executives during the proposal process. They insist that everyone propose to do the exact same thing, and they often ask for reams of mindless documentation that takes days or weeks to put together. The result is a set of nearly identical proposals that vary little in their approach, methodology, and cost. Here are a few suggestions for dealing with RFPs:

- *Don't always accept an RFP.* If you feel an RFP process will not allow you to demonstrate your uniqueness and value, and that it requires an inordinate investment of time for a limited payoff, don't participate! I know some professionals who, once they review the terms of an RFP, politely decline to submit a proposal. If the contract is for $500,000, and you are one of five competitors, you have approximately a 20 percent chance to win $500,000 in business—$100,000 if viewed on a probability-weighted basis. If your net margins are a robust 25 percent, and your probability-weighted profit is therefore $25,000, is it really worth investing $50,000 to prepare a proposal? Of course, this is the expected profit on the first go-around, so your decision to accept will hinge on whether you think the initial RFP can turn into a longer term relationship. You need to carefully assess the risk of losing money on these types of deals!

- *Define the terms in your favor.* Always try to define the terms of an RFP so that it allows you to demonstrate your strengths. If an existing client decides to issue an RFP and lets you bid on it, you should spend time with her to help clarify her needs and articulate what it is she really wants—and reflect this set of priorities in the RFP. Chances are the RFP, rather than being a one-dimensional, boilerplate document, will be more thoughtful and perhaps more focused on the kinds of services you can offer. Jerry Panas, who heads the nation's leading fundraising consulting firm, Jerold Panas, Linzy & Partners, typically gives prospective clients a comprehensive document entitled "How to Choose a Fundraising Consultant." He says, "Boards of Directors of nonprofit institutions have very little experience in choosing consultants. The checklist gives them a detailed set of criteria and includes space to score each firm on each factor. It really informs what they look for when asking for proposals from multiple firms." Obviously, Panas feels that such a comprehensive checklist is going to favor his firm, which offers a broad set of services. In any event, the checklist, which is nicely formatted and professionally printed, is perceived as a value-added service by clients.

- *Offer options.* Always include several value-added options in your proposal. I don't mean you should write three proposals. Rather, set forth your program of work, and then offer options that add more value. Author Alan Weiss calls this a "menu of yeses" that enables a client to make a choice of how to proceed rather than being forced to give a simple yes or no.[2] This range of options will differentiate you from competitors, who are unlikely to be so thorough, and it also gives clients a chance to migrate upwards and choose more value (in my experience, they often do).

- *Try to create a personal bond.* It's worth repeating: Be aggressive about trying to meet face-to-face with your prospective client during an RFP process. Too much familiarity may breed contempt, but a little bit can give you an edge!

"These days, some people will do anything to distinguish themselves."

4. Assessments

Some companies offer to do a free assessment or diagnosis for a client, betting that the problems they uncover will persuade the client to do business with them. One productivity consulting firm was notorious for this approach, offering to do a free, one-week factory productivity assessment for potential clients. Legend has it that this free assessment focused on creating terror and a fear of failure rather than a balanced picture of the client's strengths and weaknesses. However, I think that this can be a very powerful technique if it is done properly. Many firms waste their resources by not positioning such an assessment phase in the right manner. Here are some basic principles to follow:

- *Don't give it away for free.* In most cases, you should charge something for an assessment. When a client pays nothing for a product or service, it becomes devalued in his mind. Something that is "free" can also raise a client's suspicions: "If you're not charging for it, you must be the one getting the benefit!" One good approach is to offer to do this type of diagnostic phase at a shared cost. You might say, "I believe in creating long-term partnerships with my clients, and I'm suggesting that each of us make an investment in this first step. I'm willing to invest my profit margin if you are willing to invest my cost. Like partners in a business venture, we're each putting something into it at the start."

- *Focus on relationship building.* Spend as much time building a relationship with the client as you do gathering facts and analyzing them. I have seen some firms, for example, pour all their energy into creating an airtight business case that falls flat on its face because they haven't bothered to get to know each client executive's hot buttons, likes, and dislikes.

- *Start out on the right foot.* Position the assessment from day one as only the first step in creating a long-term relationship and identifying a significant issue that you're going to work on together. Don't engage in insecure behavior by constantly telling your client that she can simply walk away when you're finished if she doesn't like the result. Never forget that the purpose of the assessment is to define and launch a major engagement, not produce a stand-alone analysis for free.

The most common pitfalls associated with each of these starting points are summarized next:

Beginning a Relationship: *Common Pitfalls*

STARTING POINTS	Pitfalls
"Let's Go"	• Unclear objectives. • Lack of proper organizational buy-in. • A small piece of work pigeonholes you. • You undersell yourself in the rush to start.
Value-Added Proposal	• Not enough face-to-face meetings. • Buying influences not understood. • Emphasis on "activities" (inputs) rather than objectives and value (outputs). • No insight in the proposal.
Request for Proposal (RFP)	• Low estimated ROI based on number of competitors and expected value of bid. • Terms do not favor you. • Little or no client contact.
Assessment	• Client devalues it because you give it away. • Excessive focus on analysis rather than relationship building. • Poor positioning: "Of course you're free to turn down our ultimate proposal…"

Client relationships can begin in many ways. Whether a client simply calls and says, "Let's get going" or e-mails you a 100-page RFP, it's up to you to distinguish yourself as a cut above the crowd of experts for hire lining up at his door, and to position yourself for the long term.

In the next chapter, we'll look at five ways of growing a relationship once you're in the door.

18

Five Ways to Grow Your Client Relationships

Whether a client relationship grows or withers depends mostly on you. Are you consistently adding value by solving your client's problems and improving his business? Have you developed a trusted, personal relationship with your client? Do you consistently go the "extra mile"?

If you can answer yes to these questions, there is a very good chance you will have a client for life, or certainly someone who will strongly recommend you to others once your work is completed. In addition to implementing these principles, developing a relationship over time requires a careful strategy for growth. There are five specific growth strategies—I call them migration paths—that you can follow if you want to successfully expand your relationships. These are not "sales" strategies per se (Chapter 22 sets out some basic principles for relationship selling), but rather different routes to broadening and deepening your relationships.

1. Increase Your Market Share for Your Service

This is particularly applicable when you're dealing with a known purchasing volume and several competitors who divide up the market—this could be the case for anything from telephone switches to advertising services. Many companies are consolidating their suppliers, and the question is how to be one of the few who are left if your client travels down this road. (This trend, in turn, is leading to consolidation among service firms and other suppliers, who often have to provide a full range of services to survive as one of the finalists.)

Many books and articles have been written about ways to increase market share. My focus is on how to strengthen the client relationship. All of the breakthrough strategies described in Chapter 3 can be used to grow market share in this type of situation—for example, being easier to do business with, being faster, and more responsive.

I will highlight two particular strategies. First, build deeper personal relationships with your client and learn more about him—his strategy, his organization, and his industry—than your competitors. This depth of knowledge will ensure that you are the first to hear about his emerging needs, and it will help you come up with a steady stream of new ideas and suggestions for him. Second, develop partnering opportunities that bring you closer than arm's length. These could include codeveloping some intellectual capital; having your client outsource an activity to you, which you can do better and cheaper; providing exclusive access to your products or services; and establishing longer term contractual arrangements based on mutual cost savings and other efficiencies.

2. Migrate to New Issues Where Your Expertise Is Valuable

When you have a trusted relationship with a client, this migration can happen naturally. My personal attorney helped me with my house purchase and later did my estate planning. I assisted a client by evaluating a strategic program that was being badly implemented and later helped him assess a potential acquisition. There are several things you can do to accelerate this process:

- *Demonstrate that you are a deep generalist and not just a narrow specialist with limited expertise.* This is a subtle process that involves both push (from you) and pull (from your client). You have to constantly ask thought-provoking questions about your client's business and organization. You have to demonstrate, in your casual conversations, that you have both a curiosity and breadth of knowledge about business matters in general.

- *Illustrate your specific competency to handle other issues besides the one you've been called in to deal with.* This needs to be done subtly yet elegantly. A friend of mine who works for a large advertising agency, for example, brought a colleague who is a branding expert to lunch with a long-standing client. The client had a branding issue, but had not perceived my friend's firm as having expertise in this area.

    You can give a client an article you've written, or describe a client assignment you successfully completed in the relevant area. This evidence can testify to your credibility to do work in areas other than those you are primarily known for. Mel Immergut of Milbank Tweed, for example, organized a daylong meeting with a client and brought in several senior partners to showcase his law firm's capabilities in a new area.

- *Constantly listen and observe.* You need to create face-time with clients, walk the halls, and read and learn as much as you can about their business. When I worked with a large consulting company, I once had lunch with a European client and noticed on the way to the dining room that a conference room sign had the name of one of my firm's competitors on it. When I asked my lunch guest about it, he said, "Oh, I asked one of my people to talk with a few firms about CRM [customer relationship management] and some related technology issues we need to address." He didn't perceive me as a resource for this particular problem, but I told him that they ought to talk to my firm before making a selection. In fact, we got the job.

3. Migrate to Working for Other Executives in the Same Company

At some point, your client may no longer need your services, or he may have exhausted his budget for what you do. But in most companies of any size, there are often several other executives who could hire you. I have done assignments, for example, for the CEO, the head of marketing, and the HR director—all executives in the same company. To make this strategy work, you have to network extensively within your client's organization and get to know as many executives as possible. This is also important because it can be dangerous to place all your bets on just one client—after all, what do you do when he or she suddenly leaves?

How do you do this? Here are some suggestions:

- Early in the relationship, meet as many executives as you can from different functional areas. This interaction is critical to gathering the multiple perspectives you'll need anyway to properly inform your own work.[1]
- Halfway through the project you are working on, talk to your client about additional points of view you should solicit before reaching any final conclusions. This will serve to publicize your work and provide introductions to other key players.
- At the end of your engagement—or if you're selling a sophisticated product such as software, when the client has

taken delivery—take this as an opportunity to network and meet with other managers who are in some way affected by your product or service.

Many professionals I have worked with have a narrow definition of who their "client" is. People are surprised by how complex the influences on buying can be, especially in large organizations. Corporate purchasing and procurement managers now get involved in contracting for all sorts of services, and functional heads are more sensitive than ever to the opinions of the line executives that they serve.

By the way, if you serve individual clients (as opposed to organizations), think about the family unit as a surrogate for "the corporation." Many individual advisors, for example, have migrated from working for just one family member to serving the needs of parents, siblings, and cousins.

4. Help Your Client with Implementation

Much of the growth of professional service firms in the last 10 years, especially among consulting companies, has been based on helping clients implement the advice they've been given. It's no surprise that one of the fastest growing areas for high-technology firms is professional services, which are designed to help clients and customers properly use the equipment and software they've purchased. IBM's growth engine over the past five years, for example, has been its global services division.

These professional services can include project management, systems integration, design work, and management consulting. In addition, there are few services today that U.S. companies haven't outsourced or considered outsourcing. For your clients, the benefits can include getting the work done faster; relieving the client's managers of the burden of a temporary, burdensome, and one-off project load; and ensuring that the implementation is done properly.

Having someone take care of implementation is, for me, one of the benefits of a personal financial advisor: She gets the work done! Many of us can come up with a reasonable financial management strategy on our own—for instance, the right allocation of stocks versus bonds—but implementing that strategy and periodically adjusting it takes time, attention, and focus. These can be some of the values that a good advisor offers.

To sell implementation services to your clients, you have to do several things:

- Make it clear at the beginning that you are effective at working with clients to implement new ideas and programs.
- Learn to quantify and sell the benefits of implementation.
- Invest time to properly market this service—if it's an add-on at the end of your final presentation, your chances of winning implementation work are slim to none. Your capabilities and the client's need have to be established well before you conclude your current assignment.
- Get references from past clients that highlight your implementation work.

5. Work with Multiple Divisions of the Same Company

In consulting with the division of a large U.K. retailing company, I arranged with my client, the division head, to invite the CEO of the parent corporation to a presentation I made to the division's top 100 managers. Afterward, I met privately with the CEO to give him a personal briefing, after which he turned to me and said, "I'd like to spread this program to several of our other divisions." I ended up working with his firm for many years. This works very well for international business because each country or region can be treated like a separate business. Some years ago, for example, I developed expertise in a particular marketing program for American Express. The company's top European marketing executive introduced me to a number of regional vice presidents, and soon I found myself flying all around the world to consult on marketing strategy (this was great fun and I sampled the cuisine of over 20 countries, but the assignment severely pigeonholed me as the go-to person for a specific, narrow consulting service). Especially if you are dealing with Fortune 500 companies, this is an effective strategy for creating large accounts.

Here are a few things you need to do if you want to improve your chances of implementing a multidivisional growth strategy:

- *Have a clear methodology and approach that can be easily rolled out to other divisions.* The more custom-tailored your work—the less generalizable it seems—the harder it will be for your client to imagine it easily replicated in another part of his company. Make it easy to hire you to do the same thing elsewhere!

- *Identify forums where you can showcase your work to other division executives.* If your client has quarterly or annual meetings with his peers, offer to develop a presentation that one or both of you can give at one of these meetings.

- *If your client's organization is highly decentralized, invest the time to network on your own.* Offer to meet with other divisional managers who might have an interest in what you've done.

- *Be proactive.* Do your homework on your client's other businesses, and show how your services can produce similar or better results for them as well. Ask for a referral or recommendation!

- *Sell benefits.* You have to be able to describe, in quantitative or qualitative terms, the impact your work has already had on the company.

Growing a Relationship: *Summary*

MIGRATION PATHS	Key Enablers
Grow Market Share	• Focus early on breakthrough strategies. • Create partnering opportunities. • Develop more intimate client knowledge than your competition.
Focus on a New Issue	• Show you're a deep generalist. • Demonstrate new competencies. • Constantly listen and observe.
Work for a New Client Executive	• Network extensively at the beginning, middle, and end of your engagement.
Move into Implementation	• Discuss at the beginning–not the end– of your assignment. • Learn to quantify the benefits.
Expand to a Different Business Unit	• Package and "productize" your work so it's easy to roll-out. • Identify and invest in showcase forums with other business heads.

An excellent treatment of cross-selling, which implicitly underlies many of these growth strategies, can be found in Ford Harding's book *Cross-Selling Success*.[2]

When you think about growing a client relationship, focus on potential migration paths. Doing good work alone isn't enough—you have to develop a clear strategy for expanding your relationship with your client and spreading the gospel, as it were, to other parts of his organization.

If that sounds a tad commercial, ask yourself these questions: "Am I proud of the work I do with clients, and do I believe I add significant value to my clients' business? Am I better than my competitors?" If you can answer yes to both, then you should feel good about growing a small relationship into a large one.

19

Are Clients Meeting *Your* Expectations?

When I was a young associate with a large international consulting firm, I was given the chance to take the lead in selling and managing an important new project. That year I was under a lot of stress: My wife had just had our first child, our expenses were growing, and I was looking forward to a possible promotion—that is, if I made the kind of superhuman contribution that seemed expected of me. I was delighted to be given this opportunity, but the bloom quickly came off the rose when I realized that the client wanted about $100,000 worth of work done for less than half that amount. When I protested to the senior management of my firm, they simply said, "Do what you have to do to sell it." So I did, and the next six months of my life were hell.

I ended up working nights and weekends to complete the project while struggling to adapt to my new home life with a young baby. But the worse part of it was the client, who turned out to be, well, a bastard. I should have recognized the warning signs: Early on I observed him yelling at his own staff and acting like a small-time dictator. He was respectful enough of me at first, but as the project progressed, he became more and more demanding, treating me like a lackey who had nothing else to do in life except serve his needs. When he read a summary memo I had written, he paused halfway through, his eyes bulging. "There's a typographical error in this," he screamed at me. "This is shoddy, unacceptable work." And that was just the beginning of his merciless abuse.

Today, I would never, ever tolerate that kind of treatment. And neither should you—or even anything close to it.

We often talk about trying to meet our clients' expectations, but rarely do we think about our own needs. In fact, our professional and personal satisfaction is very much based on working with interesting, enjoyable clients who treat us with respect.

First, let's look at what we *should* expect from our clients:

- *Respect for our knowledge and experience.* This may seem obvious, but it never ceases to amaze me how often clients second-guess the professionals they hire. This happens less, I think, in professions such as law and medicine where formal certification, licensing, and a well-defined body of knowledge are standard. In fields such as management consulting, advertising, and public relations, however, clients feel freer to challenge views that are based on a complex blend of experience and judgment rather than specific statutes. (I'm not saying clients don't question their lawyers and that patients never challenge their doctors—it's a bit easier to defend your opinion, however, if you can point to a specific, supporting standard or ruling.)
- *Personal respect.* When I was starting out, some clients consistently kept me waiting for appointments and frequently cancelled or postponed them. From a professional perspective, these same clients were among the most demanding I've ever had. They took little interest in me as a person, treating me as merely an expert for hire. After completing my work for these

executives, I never solicited new projects and made no effort to continue whatever semblance of a relationship existed.

- *On-time payment.* When clients buy heavy equipment, they are used to adhering to detailed, ironclad contracts that specify payment terms and timing. When they buy services, many executives take a lackadaisical approach and figure they can pay you whenever they feel like it. The exception seems to be medical services, at least when the patient is paying directly. A psychotherapist, for example, expects and receives payment at the time of service, and no one questions this demand.

  If you work with a large firm, someone else in your organization is probably worrying about collecting the fees, but your company's year-end profits are being reduced by the carrying cost of these receivables. If you're an independent professional or have a small company, late payment of your invoices can really hurt.

  Many service professionals don't like to send invoices until the end of the month when they have completed a portion of the work. I have asked my own clients about this practice, and many have sheepishly admitted feeling the need to "demonstrate some value" to justify sending a bill. This is a self-deprecating and unfounded belief. Clients are used to receiving an invoice upon delivery of a tangible product, and paying within 30 or 45 days even if the product won't be operational or usable for months. Why shouldn't they do the same when *you* start work?

- *Respect for agreed-upon fees.* What? Isn't it enough that they pay us? There are several things that I look out for when it comes to my clients' attitude toward my fees. First, once we establish what it's going to cost, I expect the silly, demeaning jokes to end. I don't mind the positive ones—I had a client, for example, tell his subordinates, "Given the kind of money we're paying Andrew, I expect you to listen to what he has to say and give it your full consideration." But the ongoing patter—"I'd like to have lunch with you, but I'd rather buy a Corvette instead"—is demeaning and a form of harassment you should not have to tolerate.

The second behavior that is untenable is arguing with the bill after the fact. I don't mind questions or constructive discussion, but trying to reduce an invoice after the fact (assuming you've performed against the agreed-upon contract) is unexcusable. I know of one major law firm that tells clients: "If our invoice is not acceptable, pay the amount you feel comfortable with. But don't ever call us again."

Advice on this subject varies greatly depending on whom you talk to. One authority I know recommends asking for 50 percent of your fee up-front, and the second half after the first month of work—an approach that may not always be possible to implement but which eliminates this type of client complaining altogether.[1] Author David Maister recommends that if a client is unhappy with the bill, you suggest he pay an amount that he feels represents fair compensation for whatever value he did receive.[2] If you and your client are very clear about the work you're going to do right from the start, you shouldn't have many problems of this nature.

- *Interesting work.* But not all client work is interesting, you are thinking. True enough, but I want to do interesting assignments, and I'm willing to be selective, which is a key aspect of the foundational attribute I call selfless independence. When I started my consulting career in 1981, the U.S. cellular industry was just taking shape, and to apply for a license in any given geographic area each nascent cellular company had to produce a voluminous demographic analysis of the desired territory. When my firm was hired by a company wanting to acquire a cellular license, we quickly delegated the work to our group of young, smart "research analysts" who were all recent graduates of top colleges.

They did such a great job that soon more work flooded our office, and in no time we had multiple teams of these young research associates employed day and night on the deadly boring task of crunching thousands of numbers. On a Friday evening six months later, the entire group of research associates, looking more like a lynch mob than Ivy League professionals, paraded into the managing partner's spacious corner office. "We refuse to do any more cellular studies," their leader announced. The partners were appalled, but the other young associates and I laughed among ourselves, amused by the scene and pleased that someone had taken a stand against uninteresting consulting work that provided no professional growth or stimulation.

What about things you *should not* expect from clients? Here are a few to think about:

- *Your client doesn't have to become your friend.* Most professionals I know have found that a few client relationships develop into long-term friendships, but you shouldn't expect this degree of familiarity. Some clients like to be schmoozed and taken to sports events or out to dinner; others could care less. With some clients, you'll share the personal chemistry that leads to friendship, but it isn't a prerequisite to a trusted, long-term relationship.
- *Your client isn't going to praise you all the time.* It's nice when you get told what a great job you're doing, but remember that giving praise doesn't come easily to some people (just ask their spouses). Besides, you are being paid to do a great job, and some clients therefore don't feel—for better or worse—the same need to heap praise on you the way they would a volunteer worker.
- *Your client may not make an effort to stay in touch after the work is done.* This is *your* job, so don't be offended when you don't get a birthday card next year!

I expect clients to accord me professional and personal respect, to accept and pay their bills on time, and to offer me the opportunity to do interesting work that enables me to grow as a professional. Sometimes they lavish praise on me for my excellent work. Occasionally, they become my friends as well. What more could you ask for?

Are You Moving into the Inner Circle?

✔ Are you bold with your clients? Do you occasionally go against the grain and reach conclusions even when you don't have all the data that you wish you had?

✔ Do you have a doubting mind? Do you periodically question your clients' and your own basic assumptions, and reserve judgment about whether certain outcomes are good or bad?

✔ Do you wait for your clients to tell you what they need, or do you systematically invest in understanding their issues and identifying ways in which you can help?

✔ Do you rush into new contracts, or do you ensure that the foundations are in place: clear objectives, a client who can authorize the work, enough face-to-face meetings to establish trust and credibility, and a focus on work that is consistent with your abilities and desired positioning in the market?

✔ Do your clients ask you for advice and counsel on issues that extend beyond what you're ostensibly contracted to do for them?

✔ Does a significant percentage of your revenue each year come from clients you had last year?

✔ Are you conscious of the different migration paths—increasing market share, working on a new issue, working with a new client executive, doing implementation, winning business with a different business unit or department—that allow you to grow your relationships?

✔ Are you clear about what *you* expect from your clients, and do they, for the most part, meet your expectations?

PART THREE

SUSTAINING RELATIONSHIPS YEAR AFTER YEAR

20 | Sustaining and Multiplying

I recently spoke by telephone with an executive who used to work for an old client of mine. We had not talked to each other for several years, but we had a pleasant conversation catching up on our respective careers. As it turns out, he is now a top executive at a rapidly growing company. At the end of the conversation, he said, "You know, I get my top team together every quarter for an off-site planning session. Would you be interested in being a guest speaker at one of these?" Rather than feeling flattered, I first thought rather cynically, "Why hasn't this guy called me up before? He knows I'm here!"

So indeed, why didn't he get in touch? Because I did a bad job at his old employer? No—on the contrary, he told me he recalled with great enthusiasm the work I did. Because he didn't like me personally? No, he was delighted to hear from me. Actually, the answer is simple: I wasn't on his radar screen. I had dropped out of sight, and sometimes, out of sight really is out of mind.

In Chapter 5, I discussed the four phases of building relationships: affiliating, adding value, sustaining, and multiplying. In some ways, *sustaining* relationships is one of the hardest parts of our jobs. Because the demand for certain products and services is by nature periodic, you may naturally find yourself out of touch with a client for months or years at a time. Even if there is an uninterrupted demand for what you do, you face the problem of energizing and revitalizing your relationships as time goes by.

The story of my friend who never called clearly illustrates the "radar screen" theory of buying behavior. When a client has a need for something or is trying to solve a particular problem, she will often turn to the individual or firm on her radar screen *at that moment.* Now wait, you're probably saying: What about the idea of clients *for life?* Shouldn't they always call *me,* even five years later? Well, yes and no. Clients are human, and their memories fade. A well-documented decision bias, called the "recency effect," shows how we are disproportionately influenced by recent or very visible events. If we see a picture of a car wreck or a house fire in the news, immediately we tend to assign an unrealistically high probability to the same thing happening to us. Or, if our next-door neighbor sells his house for a high price, we generalize and start believing that house prices are skyrocketing everywhere. The same phenomenon can occur in business: You may have done fabulous work for me five years ago, but I just attended a conference, and there was this fellow there who had something quite interesting to say about the death of strategic planning. I may be more inclined to call *him* rather than someone I worked with years ago.

The solution is to stay on your clients' radar screen. But achieving this degree of visibility is an infinitely harder task than it was 10 or 20 years ago. The amount of marketing material, books, and magazines that cross the desk of the average top executive is simply overwhelming. Our personal time is shrinking, yet we face a growing menu of choices. This phenomenon led Seth Godin to write an interesting book entitled *Permission Marketing.*[1] Godin's thesis is that traditional advertising and marketing—what he calls "interruption marketing"—is dying, and it is being replaced with "permission marketing." We pay less and less attention to unsolicited bids for our attention—print and TV ads, direct mail solicitations, and so on. In their place is a new kind of marketing that has been *requested* by the target buyer. Simply defined, permission marketing occurs whenever we agree to receive a marketing effort someone wants to bring to us. For example, amazon.com practices permission marketing when I buy a book at the company's Web site and I am asked, "Would you like to receive notification of new books by this author?" When I then get an e-mail a year from now heralding the arrival of the author's latest tome, I am far more likely to read the e-mail and buy the new book.

So how do you stay on a past client's radar screen? First, you need to create a discipline around staying in touch. This is one of those crucial activities that are in the "Important/Not Urgent" quadrant of Stephen Covey's time management matrix.[2] The most successful professionals treat this activity almost like a daily exercise: They do a little bit each day or each week. Some consult a set of dog-eared note cards, while others use the latest contact management software. Whatever mechanisms they use, these successful advisors systematically keep in close contact with past clients.

Remember that you don't have to say in touch with *everyone*. Focus on the most important individuals (more than 10, less than 100) who can provide strong references, and use holiday cards or other means that aren't time consuming to periodically reach a broader group.

You may find any number of techniques work for you, for example:

- *Publish a regular newsletter or magazine.* Some large professional service firms, especially in the consulting industry, publish a glossy, quarterly magazine with sophisticated content. This can also be quite effective for individual practitioners as well, assuming you have something interesting to say on a regular basis. I publish a free, monthly e-newsletter, for example, called *Client Loyalty,* which I occasionally promote directly to clients and which visitors to my Web site can subscribe to. It's become widely circulated, and I have found it an excellent way of staying in touch with old clients (including the ones that got away!) as well as other members of my network. Don't underestimate, however, the time and energy it requires on a monthly or quarterly basis to produce a newsletter.

- *Write articles and books.* A book project is obviously a major undertaking, but articles may seem less daunting. Both give you an excuse to get in touch with past clients. When I publish an article or a book, I typically do a mailing to a selected group of past clients and other contacts who I feel will have interest in the subject matter.

- *Periodically send something of interest.* This is a time-tested way of staying in touch. Know your clients' interests, and constantly be on the lookout for articles or ideas that they might find useful. I have several past clients who are very interested in the Southwest, for example, and from time to time I have sent them blurbs about new hotels or cultural events in New Mexico, where I live. The online booksellers are a real boon to this type of sustaining activity. It takes almost no time to buy a book on amazon.com or bn.com and have it sent directly to your client with a note that you type into the online form. What could be easier?

- *Have lunch or dinner with an old friend.* I've always wondered about the obsession that businesspeople have for meeting over a meal, and it turns out there is a scientific basis for it. In the 1930s, the famous psychologist Gregory Razan conducted studies that showed our positive feelings about good food are transferred to the person we're with and the subject we're talking about while eating.[3] In other words, if I have a good meal with you, I am likely to feel just a bit more positive about doing business with you and more inclined to agree with your positions. (The research doesn't indicate, as far I've read, whether or not the food has to be good in order for this transference to occur; I'd play it safe, though, and choose a restaurant you know has superior food!)

The question is, what do you talk about, and what is the excuse for wanting to meet? If the client is a friend, or you've known him for many years, it's fairly easy to pick up the phone once or twice a year and say, "Let's have lunch. I'd like to catch up." If your relationship is more formal, I find that any one of several ice-breakers can work. Remember that it helps to arouse clients' *curiosity*. For example:

> "I was thinking of you because I just finished a project that has real relevancy to some of the issues I know you're grappling with. I thought it would be useful if we sat down over lunch and I shared some of the things I've learned."

> "I called because it's been ages since we spoke, and I've been doing some work that I think you'd find interesting. Why don't we get together or schedule some time in the next few weeks to talk?"

> "We haven't talked since we worked together two years ago, and I'd love to buy you lunch and catch up."

> "I just completed a research study on the relative performance of initial public offerings and I'd love to share the conclusions with you—I think you'd find them fascinating."

I recently did a workshop with a group of professionals who, at my urging, had decided to initiate a past client "call back" program. The problem was that while everyone had committed to calling at least five past clients, no one was making the calls. I asked the group, "What is keeping you from calling your old clients?" Here's what they said:

- "My clients have had their budgets cut, and they don't have money to spend right now. They don't want to hear from me."
- "I really don't know what to say."
- "It's embarrassing—they're probably going to tell me they don't want to meet."
- "It's just an awkward thing to do. I haven't spoken to some of these people in years."

After cataloguing all of the reasons why my clients were not making these calls, we actually role-played some hypothetical conversations. Soon, everyone was confident enough to agree that during the next week they would get in touch with at least a couple of past clients.

The results they reported were nothing less than spectacular. This success was not due so much to my coaching, but to the fact that their clients liked them and they had done good work in the past. So virtually everyone they called was quite receptive to having a conversation, either in person or on the phone. In fact, I received a flurry of e-mails after the session with actual copies of client responses. "Your phone call was well timed," wrote a senior executive from one large company, "and I'd like to immediately get a proposal from you for a six-country study."

- *Ask for advice.* Some people love to proffer opinions and give advice, and clients are often flattered when you call them and ask for their views on an issue. For example, I will often show one or two past clients of mine the draft of an article I'm writing and ask for some feedback. I've also shown clients collateral marketing material I'm developing to get their reactions. Often, I'll call to discuss a substantive business issue—for example, "How are you managing R&D in your firm right now? I'm doing some work with a client in this area, a company which is not competitive with you, and some interesting issues are surfacing."

When *Clients for Life* first came out, a client of mine bought 1,000 copies. He distributed them as holiday gifts to his customers, employees, and a number of financial institutions that his company worked with. In a direct sense, my client was helping to *multiply my influence,* which is the final stage of the process of building relationship capital. You might object, "I don't have a book that I can ask my clients to distribute!" Maybe not, but you have other things that can be "distributed," such as your ideas and your reputation. Here are some simple ways to multiply your influence:

- *Ask clients to pass on your ideas.* If you've published an article or newsletter, conducted some research, or written a white paper on a particular issue—ask your clients directly if they know anyone else who might be interested in reading it.
- *Ask for referrals.* Entire books have been written on this topic. Asking for a referral is awkward for many professionals because they feel it's indelicate to have to ask.[4] "You're familiar with my work and my capabilities," you might say to a past client, "and in fact I'm always looking for new clients. Could you suggest a couple of names of contacts you have who could benefit from what I do?" The best professionals I know at getting referrals are financial advisors. Because it's very hard to advertise or market this type of service, private bankers and high-end brokers have to develop their skills at getting personal introductions. One good technique is to tell a new client, as you start work with her, "My lifeblood is getting referrals from highly satisfied clients. I'm hoping that a year from now I can come to you and ask *you* to give a reference and recommend me to some of your own contacts."
- *Ask for introductions.* Old clients can serve as *catalysts* for you. These are, you will recall from Chapter 5, those individuals who make introductions and facilitate deals. A past client of yours may know someone you want to meet—it could be the head of a professional association, for example, or a board member of a company with whom you'd like to do business.

Networks facilitate exponential growth—in other words, if five of your clients each tell three people about you, and if each of them just tells one other—you've suddenly reached 30 potential new clients. This is why I believe you should make it a habit of giving away good ideas to clients instead of hoarding them until someone cracks open the checkbook. The more your ideas are spread around, the more notoriety you'll achieve and the greater the chances that someone will call you directly or be receptive when you do get in touch.

A final way of taking long-term client relationships to new levels is to partner with clients in innovative ways. Mike Mulica, the senior vice president of sales and customer field operations for Openwave Systems, the leading supplier of mobile Internet software for cell phones, describes how powerful these innovative partnerships can be:

> Early on in the development of this market a number of other large players were entering with competing products. There was a limitation on the number of companies that could really create and manufacture software for the wireless Internet environment, however, and we decided to use this fact to develop some partnerships that would create advantages for both sides. I sat down with the VP of marketing at BT (formerly British Telecom), and we mapped out a partnering arrangement that went way beyond the typical product purchasing agreement. Fundamentally, we offered BT, and they contracted for, a lock on our factory capacity for two years and a series of *as-yet unknown* product innovations in five different product categories. In other words, they bought guaranteed industry capacity and future innovation from us, all in the context of a long-term partnership. This client became our biggest advocate in the industry, and helped us to springboard our sales to other major telecommunications companies.

Your relationships with former and current clients represent a huge asset. Regular efforts to sustain, deepen, and multiply these relationships will give you one of the highest returns on investment you'll ever get, anywhere.

21 | Merlin

Working a Little Magic with Your Clients

Imagine a personal advisor completely dedicated to your success, with little regard for his own agenda—someone who is highly educated and equally skilled at helping you develop both big-picture strategies and winning tactics. Picture an advisor who, at the moment of your greatest successes, slips unnoticed into the background so that you receive all the credit. In your times of difficulty, he suddenly appears, always helping to turn the tide in your favor. Sometimes he even seems to be working a little *magic* on your behalf. Nonsense, you think—there's *nobody* around like that. Well, maybe not right now, but there used to be. This advisor was real, and his name was Merlin.

Don't laugh—read on. Some historians now believe that King Arthur's famous counselor was a real person who lived from 450 A.D. to 536 A.D.[1]

Merlin, in many respects, is the *archetypal* advisor: His qualities and character surface again and again in our history, literature, and culture. Nearly 1,500 years after his death, Merlin is a fixture in our popular culture. His exploits are the fodder for numerous Hollywood movies and television specials, and as a symbol he crops up just about everywhere. The *Star Wars* movies draw heavily on the Merlin legend: Obi-Wan Kanobi, who is Luke Skywalker's first teacher, is a Merlin look-alike, replaced later on by the enigmatic Yoda, who completes Luke's Jedi Warrior training in the wilderness. Dozens of books have been written about Merlin or borrow from his exploits. He embodies many of the qualities we seek in great advisors; in legend, he also takes on other characteristics that satisfy our many subconscious wishes and desires. The basic facts of Merlin's life can teach us much about being a great advisor.

Historians believe that Merlin was a Welsh priest, who advised not one but four kings: Yortigern, Aurelius Ambrosius, Uther Pendragon, and finally, Arthur. The stories of his exploits were handed down through oral tradition; it was not until about 1200 that they were finally written down. The legends about Merlin were obviously very powerful, as they became quite widespread and were eventually recorded by many different cultures in multiple languages, including English, Latin, and French.

Merlin was born around 450 in what is now Wales. Legend has it that his mother was a mortal woman and his father a demon and that he was extremely precocious from birth. His first "consulting" assignment came at age six, when a local king was having problems building his new castle. Every time the castle walls were erected, they fell to the ground. Advisors told the king that he must sacrifice a young boy to ensure successful completion of the building. Merlin was chosen for the sacrifice and brought before the king. Merlin spoke up rather cheekily and told the king, "Your advisors have told you to sacrifice a young boy, but they haven't answered the question *why* the walls collapse." Merlin continued, "Dig down under the foundations of the castle. There, you will find an underground river. Divert it, and you will be able to build the castle." Sure enough, the king had his men dig, and they found the hidden waters. Even at age six, Merlin demonstrated conviction in the face of overwhelming authority, and he was able to reframe the king's problem by asking a provocative question.

Merlin grew up and lived in the woods. He built a hideaway near the Welsh seacoast, far up on a cliff (recalling Batman's cave or Superman's fortress of steel at the North Pole). Years later, after the Romans left England and returned to their disintegrating empire in the south of Europe, Merlin realized that a great leader was needed to organize the Celts against the invading Saxons. He hatched a plan to take a baby with a strong genetic inheritance—the future Arthur—and train him to be a great king.

Naturally, the right baby was born, Merlin appeared, and he whisked the baby off to his hideaway. There, for the next 15 years, he educated Arthur and trained him in the arts of war and state-hood. Merlin then arranged for the sword Excalibur to be placed in a stone, to set up the first "proof" that Arthur should be king. The young boy successfully pulled the sword out, and he became king. Merlin remained close by as his most trusted advisor.

Whenever Arthur got into trouble, Merlin appeared. If it was during a battle with the Saxons, a red dragon—Merlin's symbol—appeared over the battlefield, just as Batman projected the bat symbol over the Gotham City skyline. This sight rallied Arthur's troops and presaged Merlin's imminent arrival to save the day. Interestingly, according to tales of his exploits, Merlin gave Arthur rather specific advice: "Send a detachment of soldiers to a spot two miles down the river from here," Merlin told Arthur, helping him to set up an ambush. Then, he helped Arthur lay out a master plan for the battle.

Merlin exemplified virtually all of the qualities that character-ize great advisors. He had a *learning attitude,* constantly studying and reading; he developed an enormous *depth and breadth of knowledge* (from literature through warfare), and instilled this in his pupil; he was skilled at both grand strategies and short-term tactics; his *judgment* was always keen—in fact, it was Merlin who con-ceived of the idea for Arthur's round table, whose design was in-tended to overcome the problems of hierarchy and preference that many of the knights held fast to; and he assiduously built *trust* with Arthur, always putting the king's agenda first.

In terms of his relationship with Arthur, he was *selfless,* preferring to fade into the woods when victory was at hand (actually, he frequently disguised himself when doing good deeds), yet he was also completely *independent*—he lived on his own far away from Arthur's castle and never accepted payment for his services. Merlin was *discrete,* never using his relationship with Arthur or special knowledge of the king to further his own ambitions. He also had absolute *conviction* about his views; indeed, he was rarely swayed by others' opinions. Merlin also adhered to a set of higher principles—freeing the north country from the Saxon invaders, for example, was a higher calling than serving any one client.

"By making our competitors disappear, Radu eliminates the need for pesky things like leadership and strategy."

In some versions of the myth, Merlin's aging process was reversed once he became an old man, and he subsequently grew younger each day. There is some useful symbolism here: In our work with long-standing clients, we have to approach each meeting, each encounter, with renewed freshness and vigor. We have to bring the same invigorated enthusiasm and new ideas to the hundredth meeting that we brought to the first one when we were wooing that client. We have to treat every long-standing client like a brand-new one.

Become a little more Merlin-like in your work with clients. You don't have to wear a wizard's cap or live in a hideaway in the woods. Focus on developing the behaviors and attributes that Merlin exemplified so well, and your own clients will start feeling as lucky as Arthur did to have such a magical advisor.

22

Five Steps to New Business with Old Clients

In any given year, many companies derive 70 percent to 80 percent of their revenues from clients and customers they did business with the year before. Among established firms, the vast amount of *selling* in business actually takes place within the context of existing relationships. This doesn't mean that acquiring new clients isn't an essential task; new clients are crucial for both financial and intellectual growth, and your ability to add value increases with the diversity of your client experiences. Your current relationships, however, usually represent your largest short-term potential to develop new revenue at a low sales cost.

There are two schools of thought about relationship selling. One says that if you simply do a great job, you'll be asked back again. Under this philosophy, there's actually no need to "sell" to existing clients: Just do good work or supply great products, and the orders will subsequently roll in. A second school argues that you must aggressively exploit your existing relationships. In a sense, you are *constantly* selling.

The best approach is somewhere in-between. Because they are so competitive, most markets don't permit us the luxury of sitting back and waiting for the phone to ring. On the other hand, clients today feel oversold-to. The frustrated client of one large accounting firm, for example, felt relentless pressure from his auditor to buy additional tax and consulting services. Exasperated, he finally asked his outside audit partner, "Are you my auditor or my salesman?"[1] George Fisher, the former chairman and CEO of Eastman Kodak Company, put it this way during a discussion I had with him about the importance of trusted advisors: "Some of the outside professionals I have used focus on adding value the whole time they are working; others are in there aggressively trying to sell the next project, which is just irritating."

If you do the things that create long-term client loyalty—if you add value, build personal trust, and go the extra mile—you will be well positioned to develop new business within your existing relationships. There are two typical mistakes that professionals make, however. First, they don't actually build a relationship with their client. They focus on being a good supplier of services but then neglect or underestimate the second part of the loyalty equation—trust. Second, they ignore the fact that whether they are selling to a brand-new client or to a client they've known for years, five building blocks need to be in place.

To sell a complex service such as consulting or investment banking, or a sophisticated product such as enterprise software, you need to establish all five. Regardless of how long the client has known you, the following five points are essential:

1. Build trust and credibility.
2. Identify the real problem.
3. Determine the impact of fixing the problem.
4. Propose a solution.
5. Close.

There are many excellent selling "systems" that have been developed over the years. Some of them are highly complex, with bells and whistles such as six-by-six matrices you have to fill out. In the end, though, they all boil down to these five basic principles.

Occasionally you can hit all of them in one meeting; sometimes it might take 10 meetings. You may feel that the process is "different" for you or your particular type of business, but in reality these are universal stages. If you want to be an advisor who delivers solutions rather than plain-vanilla expertise, you need to think in terms of these five basic points.

Whether we're talking about software, advertising, consulting, or legal services, clients buy products and services to solve a problem or resolve a business issue they have. They feel most comfortable buying from people they trust and who are credible. If what you sell costs clients a large amount of money—and you're probably not reading this book unless that's the case—they won't buy from you unless they believe they are receiving value in excess of the price they pay. So you have to demonstrate, in some way, the value of what you're doing. Finally, no one buys unless you present a concrete proposal and close.

These five principles, as you can see, are intuitively natural, essential phases of the buying process. The art lies in the nuanced way in which you accomplish them. When you have a long-standing relationship with a client, the entire process will look and feel differently, but close analysis will show that you've still touched each of these bases.

1. Build Trust and Credibility

In Chapter 4, I discussed how to build trust in the first meeting with a client, how to communicate integrity and competency—and how to reduce a client's risk of trusting you—while building face-to-face rapport. If you're already working with a client, perhaps you feel this is a superfluous step since you have already established trust and credibility through your prior work. Don't take this step for granted, however. Remember that a key element of trust is a client's perception of your competence to do a certain task. You may have built trust with a client based on a certain service you've *already* provided, but not for something *new* that you are now proposing. Furthermore, you may be talking to a new executive within the same organization, and while you will benefit from positive association (described in Chapter 7), your new contact still has to find a comfort level with you.

Building trust and credibility is an ongoing process in your relationships. Here are some reminders for achieving these qualities:

- Throw away all those PowerPoint slides extolling you and your firm. Remember my client in Chapter 4, Michael, who dragged his presentations around like a ball-and-chain? At best, these should be a "leave-behind" after a face-to-face meeting. If you make a presentation, it should always be about your client—his problems and issues—not about you.

- Establish credibility by asking good questions and by presenting brief examples of how you've helped other clients with similar issues. This is important whether the client knows you well or has just met you. In less than 200 words, a case study should describe the client's issue, your solution, and the benefits to the client. Good questions then provoke deeper thinking, uncover key issues, and demonstrate your knowledge of a client's business and industry.

- If it's a new client within the same organization, discuss your prior work for the company to create a positive association. If someone he or she trusts also trusts you, the battle is half won.

- If you work for a firm, bring in other experts to demonstrate competence in the new issue being discussed.

2. Identify the Problem

Sometimes the problem is very straightforward, and a client simply wants someone to fix it. Other times, a major part of the value you add is helping a client clarify what the real issues are. Why isn't it as easy as asking clients, "Tell us what the problem is?" It's not so simple, for several reasons.

Often clients think they know what the problem is, but they really don't. One client says, "We lack brand awareness" but the culprit is poor product quality. Another wants to launch a huge reengineering project to reduce costs, but his executive team hasn't bought into the company's strategy and vision.

Moreover, clients frequently confuse symptoms with root causes. Indeed, one of the hallmarks of great advisors is their ability to distinguish causes from effects and to go after real problems rather than proposing a band-aid solution to cover up an unsightly blemish. For example, attrition is a *symptom* of low employee morale. On the other hand, poor front-line supervision is a *problem* that may be causing that low morale.

Clients may have a problem, but it may not be causing them enough pain to justify paying you to do something about it. So it's critical to probe not just for the real problem, but to verify *how much pain* it's causing. For example, you might ask:

- "I understand that attrition is very high. What's that costing your organization?"
- "Sales are flat, and your traditional customer base is aging. What kind of impact do these conditions have on the bottom line?"
- "Have there been efforts to solve this problem using internal resources?" (If something is really a problem, usually an organization has struggled with it before calling in an outsider.)
- "If we don't do this work within the deadline you're suggesting, what do you think the costs will be?"
- "You've been managing your own investments for the last five years. Do you feel you have achieved your goals?"

3. Determine the Impact of Fixing the Problem

To motivate a client to fix a problem, you have to get him to weigh the pain that problem is causing against the benefits he imagines would result if it were fixed. Dick Carlson, a consultant and author who trains professionals in solution selling, puts it this way: "Before a client will buy, there has to be either problem impact or results impact in evidence. A client may complain about something to you, but unless he can articulate either the pain it's causing or the results that resolving it will achieve, he won't ultimately pay you to fix it."

Some pundits call this "envisioning the future" or creating a "future state vision." The point is that you need to help your client envision a future state where her problems are solved. Often, I think it's more practical and useful to ask the simple question, "What is the value of fixing this problem?" Here are some typical phrasings that will help you get to this information:

- "If you successfully solved this problem, what would the organization look like a year from now?"
- "What do you think is the value of fixing this problem?"
- "What kinds of benefits would you expect from a good solution to this matter?"
- "Once the strategy you've described is fully implemented, how will your business be different?"
- "If this merger or deal goes through, what results do you expect?"

4. Propose a Solution

If you haven't built trust and credibility, identified the real problem and the degree of pain it's causing, and assessed the impact of fixing the problem, your client isn't very likely to buy anything from you. But if you propose a solution too early in this process, you can lower your success rate significantly. Many professionals jump quickly to what they sell rather than trying to understand their client's needs and issues. Why? We're trained that way, and it feels safe. It's much easier to sell only black Model T cars, as Henry Ford did, than to spend the time digging into what customers really want in a car. Shortly after making his famous statement that consumers "can have my cars any way they want, as long as they're black," Ford was eclipsed by General Motors, which offered its customers vehicles in bright colors.

Clients also contribute to this phenomenon. Some now want the "elevator pitch," a 30-second attempt to "sell them" on your product or service. If you're in a long-term relationship, you are less likely to receive such a ridiculous request. The truth is, however, that we live in media-driven culture that thrives on the sound bite, and you do need to be able to describe what you do in one or two sentences. You need to clearly describe a *benefit* that clients receive—for example, "I help clients revitalize declining brands"; "We improve long-term business performance"; or, "I help medium-sized companies gain access to private equity financing."

Don't let yourself be forced into the elevator pitch. Describe what you do, and then add, "We tailor our work to each individual client, and if we can meet to explore your business's particular issues, I'll then be able to describe exactly how we can help and what the benefits would be to you."

When proposing a solution, you should always present it as a draft. It's best to do this in person, where it provides an opportunity for the client to "put his fingerprints" on the approach. Never send a letter that is a final proposal if you haven't already discussed it with the client.

5. Close

Has this ever happened to you? You've moved through the four steps I've described. You've formalized your proposal in a crisp engagement letter. Your client is enthusiastic about starting the work—next week, in fact. He's ready to commit to a major contract. Suddenly, silence. You don't hear back for a week—or a month. Anxious, you call. "Well, this has to go through an approval process involving our chief financial officer and vice president for operations," he tells you, adding, "But I'm optimistic they're going to like this a lot." Nobody ever mentioned these other executives!

When something untoward happens at the end of the business development process, it's usually because one or more of the first four steps haven't been properly completed. Typical pitfalls include:

- It turns out that the problem isn't serious enough to warrant paying your fees.
- The problem is owned by a different executive than the one you are talking to.
- The client is unable to articulate the real pain that the problem is causing him.
- The value of solving the problem hasn't been identified, so the client doesn't feel it's worth the investment.
- You've never talked to the "economic buyer"—the person who can say "yes" to hiring you—and when presented with the project, he or she declines, having never met you and never understood the value of the work.
- You are in a complex sale that includes many constituencies (e.g., the CEO, COO, or other line managers) and you haven't met all the key players and understood their perspectives, determined their hot buttons, and sold them on the value of the work.

Often, the client will close the engagement himself": "Okay, this looks good, so when can you start?" (Don't we wish more said that?) Sometimes, you have to force the issue:

- "Do you have all the information you need to make a final decision?"
- "Would a start date of June 1 make sense for your organization?"
- "Is there anything else we need to do to enable your organization to make a final decision on going ahead with this work?"
- "Is there anything I need to know about your organization and its people before implementing this solution?"

- "Are you able to authorize this expenditure, or does that come from elsewhere? If so, it would probably make sense for us to talk to the person who handles that budgetary line; that way, he'll have a first-hand sense of who we are and of the impact this work will have."

As I mentioned in Chapter 18, what motivates a client to buy from you in the later stages of the relationship can be somewhat different than what motivates him at the beginning. When a client first decides to do business with you, it's often based on the perception that you have new ideas, a new approach, or a hot product to offer. Later on, other factors come into play: the innovation you're able to offer that is tailored to the client's business; partnership arrangements; risk-sharing; and the insight and wisdom you can bring based on an intimate knowledge of the company's strategy and its management talent.

As you can see, careful questioning is at the heart of uncovering the exact dimensions of a client's need. An excellent treatment of this can be found in SPIN Selling by Neil Rackham, which presents a taxonomy of four types of questions—situation, problem, implication, and need-payoff—that you need to employ at different points in the selling process.[2]

Ultimately, to develop new business within an existing relationship you must become as knowledgeable as possible about your client's issues. This knowledge includes a thorough understanding of his organization, an extensive investment in networking and meeting other buyers, and the development of industry expertise. Then, you need to integrate these discussions (problem, desired result, solution) into your day-to-day work with an existing client.

In practice, it can be helpful to invest in additional meetings to discuss your findings and stimulate a client's thinking about interconnected issues that need resolution. Midway through the current project, take an assessment of the client's needs and make a new proposal now, not at the end. The most pathetic sight in the world for a client is an outside professional who, at his final presentation, makes a surprise, desperate stab at getting follow-on business! If you start the problem/result/solution cycle during your *last* meeting with a client, you'll have a delay of typically weeks or months, even if you are successful, before getting new work. Finally, if you work in a large firm, expose your client to the full range of capabilities that you and your colleagues offer. Remember, trust depends in part on a client's belief in your *competence,* so you need to manage that perception.

It's important to remember that client needs evolve and change over time, and if you want to be able to effectively serve clients for the long term, you've got to demonstrate versatility. If you're purely a one-trick pony, you will find yourself working with clients on a very periodic basis. At both the firm and individual level there is great utility in having at least several core areas of strength; even boutiques need some breadth if they want to have staying power. This is useful not just for serving an individual client over the long term, but also for diversifying your market risk—if you only appeal to one narrow segment of clients, and that market goes south, you're going to be in trouble.

At best, the relationship selling process should be almost seamlessly woven into the fabric of your day-to-day client interactions. You add great value, build personal trust, and go the extra mile. You listen carefully and constantly look around for ways to help and problems you can solve. You meet other potential buyers within the organization. Your client may come to you with a particular issue, or you may propose one to him. You help him articulate the pain the problem is causing and the expected benefits of fixing it. You may explore partnering in a way that deepens the relationship and benefits both sides. You draft an approach and agree to begin work. At this point, both you and your client are experiencing the benefits of a long-term relationship.

23 | The Rothschild Bankers

The Power of Unique Capabilities

In 1813, England's Duke of Wellington was waging war against both Spain and France, and he was in a pickle. "An army marches on its stomach," Napoleon had said, and Wellington was running out of money to buy food and supplies for his far-flung troops on the continent. "Unless this army should be assisted with a very large sum of money at a very early period," he wrote, "it will be quite impossible for me to do anything."[1] If he couldn't pay his soldiers, they would plunder the local towns, which would be a political disaster for the English.

Two problems had to be surmounted: First, Wellington needed large loans, and second, he needed huge quantities of gold and silver coins distributed to his troops all over continental Europe, an enormous logistical undertaking. The British government, despite its size and advanced financial system, lacked the resources to meet

Wellington's need. So whom did he turn to? Only one institution in the world had the means to finance the English army and ensure its payroll was met with the right currencies in multiple countries: the Rothschild banking family.

Nathan Rothschild, who ran the family's English bank, had assiduously cultivated a relationship with John Charles Herries, now the English Commissary-in-Chief. In this moment of crisis, Herries turned to Nathan and asked for his help. With merchant banking houses in five major European financial centers—London, Paris, Frankfort, Vienna, and Naples, which were run by Nathan, James, Solomon, Amschel, and Carl, respectively—the Rothschild family had in effect become a global bank. Over the next two years, it handled the financing of England's extensive war efforts. The Rothschilds took English sterling, converted it into gold and silver coins in various currencies, and arranged for transport to the battlefields where Wellington's troops were dispersed. The English prime minister, Lord Liverpool, later wrote to a friend, "I do not know what I should have done without him last year."[2] As they had many times before—and would do again in the future—the Rothschilds were able to solve financial problems that no other bank could touch.

The Rothschild dynasty was started by Mayer Amschel Rothschild, who was born in the Frankfort Jewish Ghetto in 1744. At that time, Jews had few rights in Germany or elsewhere. They were not entitled to citizenship, and in Frankfort they had to live in an unbelievably cramped neighborhood—a ghetto—which was walled off from the rest of the city. Mayer Amschel got his start as a dealer in antique coins. Early on, he built a clientele of affluent aristocrats—including William IX, who headed the wealthy German state of Hesse-Kassel—who would later become banking clients. It was natural to occasionally extend credit to his coin customers, and by the late 1790s Mayer Amschel had expanded into an array of financial services.

How Mayer Amschel actually did this is instructive. His real breakthrough came when he graduated from just extending credit to coin clients to participating in the buying and selling of English bills.

This was facilitated by the friendship he cultivated with a man named Karl Friedrich Buderus, who had worked for William of Hesse-Kassel as a tutor. Buderus moved rapidly through the ranks of William's civil servants, and ended up in his financial administration. In 1796, Buderus successfully recommended that Mayer Amschel be allowed to bid with other established firms for a block of English bills that William was selling. Buderus later became, in strategic selling terminology, Mayer Amschel's "coach." On several occasions he provided tips to Mayer Amschel on how much he should pay for notes in order to underbid the competition, and although some of this business was unprofitable, it gave the Rothschild patriarch an entree into a much bigger league than he had previously been playing in.

When the French invaded Hesse-Kassel, Mayer Amschel was one of several friends who hid and protected William's wealth. Although this story was later wildly exaggerated—Mayer Amschel had only a minor role in preserving William's fortune—it became a myth propagated by the family itself by way of underscoring the Rothschilds' "exceptional probity as deposit-holders" and the fact that they would "risk everything rather than fail to protect and pay interest on a client's money."[3]

Mayer Amschel had five sons who initially were primarily in the business of exporting textiles from England. Over time they moved into financial services and merchant banking activities. By the time Nathan, his eldest son, died in 1836, the Rothschilds were the wealthiest family in the entire world. In the space of only a few decades, Mayer Amschel and his five sons had created, relatively speaking, the most powerful financial institution in history. Neither the house of Morgan in the late-nineteenth century, nor any of today's largest banks, has come close to achieving the influence and power wielded together by the five Rothschild banking houses.

Several notable factors—all quite relevant to modern professionals—contributed to their success:

1. *A relentless emphasis on relationship-building*. By successfully cultivating relationships with government officials like

Buderus, Mayer Amschel successfully leveraged the early client re-lationships he built in his antique coin business into much larger ones. He did whatever it took—including sharply discounting his fees—to capture business with high-profile royalty in his home country of Germany. After his death, his five sons frequently re-membered his advice about building key relationships, quoting it frequently in letters to each other (for example, "When he had oc-casion to apply to an inferior or a man who had little power to as-sist him in carrying an object he had in view, [Father] spoke with the person as if the whole depended entirely on him, though per-haps he knew he had but the smallest possible influence in the busi-ness").[4] Mayer Amschel was skilled at making even the lowliest clerk feel important.

Because much of the Rothschild banking business involved government loans and bonds, intelligence on political events was crucial to the family's success. The five brothers cultivated gov-ernment officials at the highest levels, sometimes lending them money or letting them participate in deals, and they built lavish homes throughout Europe in which they entertained the political elite. James Rothschild once wrote, speaking about his brother in London, "Nathan's relations with these gentlemen [of the Trea-sury] is such between brothers."[5] Not all of these practices would be appropriate today, but the focus on building relationships and gaining intelligence is still of utmost importance for contemporary client advisors.

2. *A close-knit partnership based on mutual trust.* Few family businesses last more than one or two generations, but the Roth-schilds' has endured, in one form or another, for nearly 200 years. Despite many opportunities for disagreement and schisms, the five sons worked together in relative harmony for decades. In Chapter 27, you'll read about how rain-making firms engage in trust-building activities that not only reassure clients but enable their pro-fessional staff to work together in the best interests of clients. The Rothschild brothers achieved this trust-building in spades.

Biographer Niall Ferguson writes, "If there was a single 'secret' of Rothschild success it was the system of co-operation between the five houses."[6] Prime Minister Benjamin Disraeli remarked at the time, "The prosperity of the Rothschilds was as much owing to the unity of feeling which alike pervaded all branches of that numerous family as in their capital & abilities."[7] Every few years, the five brothers fine-tuned their partnership agreements so that each knew where he stood and what he might expect. The brothers trusted each other completely, and this mutual confidence enabled them to freely act on each other's behalf during even the most sensitive, high-stakes negotiations.

3. *Unique sources of information.* The Rothschilds had three unique sources of information that enabled them to add value to their clients and also make profits for their own accounts. First, they maintained a network of salaried agents in all of the world's stock markets. These agents wrote daily dispatches to the five main Rothschild houses, informing them of the latest news and developments. Second, the Rothschild brothers cultivated relationships with politicians around the world, especially in England, the European Continent, and Russia. Finally, they occasionally used a network of carrier pigeons to ensure that they had the absolute latest news about important events such as war and revolution. Use of these pigeons allowed the Rothschilds in London to learn about Wellington's victory over Napoleon at Waterloo well before the English government did.

4. *A mission oriented to their Jewish identity.* A fourth element of the Rothschilds' success was the fact that they embraced and retained their strong Jewish identity. In the nineteenth century, it was quite common for wealthy Jews to convert to Christianity in order to become accepted into mainstream society. Many of the Rothschilds' banking rivals followed this route, abandoning their heritage in exchange for societal acceptance. Anti-semitism was rife at the time, and being Jewish was a significant impediment to financial

and social success. One factor that distinguishes great client advisors is a mission orientation, and the Rothschilds were driven by a deep commitment to their heritage and faith. An important piece of their personal mission was to raise the lot of Jews. They consistently used their vast wealth and connections to improve the status of Jews throughout Europe, lobbying hard for citizenship rights and other forms of recognition they had been denied. Their closeness as siblings, no doubt, was also enhanced by their sense—very much based in reality—of being a besieged minority.

5. *Innovative client solutions.* Nathan Rothschild, who set up the family's English branch, could have easily written the chapter on breakthrough client strategies. When he started the family's textile export business, based in Manchester, he always pushed to offer his clients a better value proposition than his competition. He cut out the middleman, and by going directly to suppliers in remote areas of the British Isles, he was able to offer lower prices. He ensured he had the largest variety of patterns. He organized the fastest means of shipment. Later, as a banker, Nathan was always able to do something unique for clients, and make hefty profits for himself and his family to boot. Because of their interconnected operations in so many financial centers, the Rothschilds were able to undertake transactions—such as the financing of Wellington's army—that no one else could touch. Similarly, their grasp of exchange rate fluctuations were such that they could usually turn a tidy profit on the transactions they conducted for clients, at lower risk than the competition. Because of their unique sources of information, they were able to offer clients the most current information on the financial markets and the political events that drove them.

The Rothschilds, in short, were extraordinarily adept at building their relationship capital and then leveraging it through their proprietary information and interlocking banking operations across

Europe. It's instructive to compare the Rothschilds with the Jesuits, whom we looked at in Chapter 12. The two certainly fell at opposite ends of the religious spectrum: devoted Jews, on the one hand, versus arch-Catholics, on the other—but they actually had many important qualities in common. Both were deep generalists—the Jesuits were trained to undertake any task, anywhere, and the Rothschilds were broadly talented businessmen as opposed to narrow financial specialists. Both enjoyed an enormous sense of internal cohesion based on high standards that engendered mutual trust and a mission orientation. Mentoring was important to both: Recall the Jesuits' formal process for mentoring called the "account of conscience"; and in a similar vein, the five Rothschild brothers carefully tutored and developed their young nephews, preparing them to take their places in running the family business. Both also had, to differing degrees, a mission focus—the Jesuits determined to spread the word of God and the will of the Pope, the Rothschilds deeply concerned with using their wealth to improve the condition of Jews. Although the Rothschilds were not altruistic client advisors along the lines of a Sir Thomas More or General George Marshall, we can still learn important lessons from their success at cultivating and serving the needs of powerful clients.

Nathan Rothschild was the first of Mayer Amshel's sons to die, and his demise in 1836 rocked the financial markets around the world more severely than the outbreak of a major war. The family business went forward, however, and even today some of Mayer Amschel's direct descendants are involved in international finance.

24

Cultivating the Attitude of Independent Wealth

What I'm about to describe is one of the most powerful things you can do to attract and keep clients. If you are successful at it, you'll create a perceptible aura around you that is enormously attractive not only to clients but to anyone with whom you have a business relationship. It doesn't cost anything, and the implementation is entirely up to you. Sound easy? It is—sort of.

Here goes: One of the secrets of building long-term client loyalty is to behave with clients as if you're not getting paid. That's right, work 60 or more hours a week, hustle to meet deadlines, and lie awake at night wondering if there's any flaw in the project you just completed—and then pretend you're doing it for free. "Ridiculous," someone once said to me after I had recommended this during a speech. "My firm needs to make a profit, and clients should pay for our services," he told me afterwards, having interpreted my advice a bit too literally. Indeed, he was right—you need to charge clients fair fees for your services, send out bills on time, and do all of the other things that make you profitable. But when you're with a client, you can't have the meter running in your head. You have to exude enjoyment and enthusiasm for what you do and treat the client like a friend. No matter how skinny your bank account, you have to convey the semblance of independent wealth.

The opposite of the attitude of independent wealth—let's call it the scent of greed or scarcity—is repugnant to clients, and they can smell it a mile away. A colleague once described to me the training program he went through many years ago at a large brokerage firm. When cold-calling prospective clients, he was taught to envision, just before picking up the phone, the yacht or expensive sports car he would buy with his year-end bonus. When I told this story to a friend of mine who is a well-known financial advisor, he exclaimed, "Good grief! This fellow was being taught to visualize greed!"

Developing an attitude of independent wealth is an excellent way to cultivate *selfless independence,* which is one of the foundational qualities of great client advisors that I described in Chapter 2. Arguably, many of the biggest corporate scandals of the last decade have had at their roots a systematic lack of independence on the part of virtually everyone involved, including the professional service firms hired by these companies, senior management, and the boards of directors.

Throughout history, we have admired individuals who are truly independent. The legendary Cincinnatus, for example, was the Roman soldier who took a few days off from his farm to lead the rescue of a besieged Roman army in 458 B.C.. He then refused entreaties to become emperor for life and instead returned to his pastures. Thomas More famously stood up to his client, Henry VIII, and was beheaded when he refused to give up his independence and endorse, against all his principles, Henry's divorce and the split with the Catholic Church. Our admiration for this quality applies to every field: In sports, for example, the boxer Muhammad Ali took on the establishment with an independence of spirit that initially enraged entrenched interests like the Mafia (which ran boxing in those days) and the boxing regulatory authorities. When the

Supreme Court finally overturned his conviction for draft dodging—Ali had refused on religious grounds to be drafted for service in Vietnam—he was free to don his boxing gloves again and win the heavyweight championship. Thereafter, he rose to the status of national hero and today is one of the most famous and widely recognized Americans outside the United States.

"Our approach? It's rigorous and independent. We ask our clients what they want to do, and then advise them to do it."

So how do you cultivate the mind-set of independent wealth? It's not easy, at least not in the context of Western culture. We live in a society that seeks wealth and the trappings of wealth—a trophy home, new cars, and exotic vacations. Furthermore, we want to win at any cost, and we have instilled this desire in our children (in a recent study of 4,500 teenagers by Rutgers University, 75 percent of them admitted to serious cheating at school).[1] All this materialism runs counter to building the inner confidence and strength that underpin a sense of personal rather than monetary wealth. That said, here are some suggestions to explore:

- *Make sure you are doing work that you love.* In his book, *Making a Life, Making a Living,* Mark Albion talks about having finally found work that is so rewarding and enjoyable that he cannot distinguish between "work" and "play" anymore.[2] When someone asked him how many hours a week he works, he replied, "How many hours a week do I breathe? I don't count my work hours because I can't really distinguish between those hours and any others."

- *Think often about the people who are most important to you.* Reflect on how wealthy you are in terms of the relationships in your life. I remember being thrown into an absolute panic years ago by an incident with a major client that occurred while I was living in Europe. My mother, who happened to be visiting at the time, watched me reach the boiling point and almost collapse with anxiety. On a walk one evening, she said to me, "You know, in 10 years you won't even be able to recall why you were so upset this week. But your family and close friends will still be with you. They are what counts." And you know what? Today I can barely remember the conflict with the client, and I deeply regret the turmoil I caused my family during those days.

- *Rationally evaluate the importance and impact of losing a client or missing a sale.* I ask myself two questions when confronting news that could potentially shake my sense of independence and my confidence: First, does this event pose a physical or emotional threat to my family or me? Second, will it have a serious, long-term effect on my career and professional life? If I cannot answer "Yes" to one or both of these questions, then it's simply not worth getting agitated. How often does a setback with a client pass this test? You guessed it: It's never happened to me even once.

- *Think about how you would spend your time if you didn't have to work for money.* Warning: This is a risky exercise! An even more dangerous corollary is to ask yourself: If you were not currently with your spouse or significant other, would you choose that person again right now to be with for the rest of your life? If your answer is that you'd do the exact same work you're engaged in now, you're lucky and have 100 percent alignment between work and play. If they don't coincide, think about how you might slowly begin to add more of the activities and pursuits that you wish you could have more of or would prefer to do. Even a small move in this direction will greatly increase your sense of personal wealth, regardless of the remuneration.

■ *Spend more time developing your physical and mental self in ways that are unrelated to your client work.* I play guitar, for example, and find that my late-night sessions help create a healthy escape from the ups and downs of my professional practice. Physical activity, be it just a walk in the foothills around my house or a day skiing with my wife, also "un-hooks" me from work and contributes to a centeredness that gives me an independence vis-à-vis my clients.

For those of you who feel that this chapter is a bit soft or self-helpish for your taste, just recall the words of a well-known CEO, Charles Lillis, who said this to me about outside advisors: "I wish all of my professional advisors were independently wealthy. They would then be objective, independent, and less likely to be pushing their own agenda."[3] Although few clients could articulate this concept as well as this particular executive, they all recognize it when they see it. It boils down to having complete intellectual honesty with your clients—which means always telling them the way you really see things; putting their interests and well-being ahead of your personal financial gain; and cultivating your own inner confidence. If you do this—and don't forget to send out your bills while you're at it—you'll experience wealth of all sorts over the long term.

25 | Managing Client Relationships during Uncertain Times

During the economic boom of the late 1990s, there was such demand for certain services that some businesses routinely turned clients away. Every new dot-com startup, for example, wanted publicity and brand awareness. Public relations firms experienced an unprecedented surge in demand. Some consulting firms and investment banks began asking for not only their normal fees but also equity "kickers" in the form of stock or options in their clients' company. "If we're going to put our reputation on the line and help one of these companies gain access to capital," one prominent lawyer told me during this period, "then, sure, we ask for a piece of the action *in addition to* our full fees." Alas, all good things must pass.

As you read this book, the economy may be robust or faltering. The business outlook may be bullish or bearish. One thing is for sure, however: At some point you will have to deal with managing clients in an environment of great uncertainty. During uncertain times, what needs to change in terms of how you go about acquiring new clients and managing your ongoing relationships? The nice thing about managing client relationships using time-tested principles is that you can rely on them through thick and thin—economic or political uncertainty shouldn't affect your basic approach. Add great value, build a trusted personal relationship, and go the extra mile— these fundamental building blocks of client loyalty don't change with the ups and downs of the stock market or with changes in interest rates.

When times are difficult, what often holds us back is our own attitude. The old truism that we are our own worst enemies came to life for me recently when, as a student of Japanese Shotokan karate, I entered a tournament. During a training session for the sparring event, several of us were nervously pumping our teacher with questions that were fundamentally rooted in insecurity: "What if the other guy charges right off the line?" "What if she's faster than I am?" "What's the best way to block a spinning hook kick?"

The sensei replied quite simply, "When you go into the match, you are not fighting your opponent so much as yourself." My teacher's point was that we overestimate our competition, underestimate our own abilities, and allow fear slow us down or even paralyze us.

The same thing happens in business. We are held back by numerous assumptions, beliefs, and attitudes that, when taken together, form myths about the managing of client relationships in uncertain times:

Myth: *"My clients just don't want to see me."*

Many businesspeople think that their clients don't want to see them when the economy is doing poorly, reasoning that if a client doesn't have any money to spend, he doesn't want to be "sold" to. This attitude says more about the mind-set of the professional than the client. In reality, your clients need you more than ever during times of crisis—their issues are more complex and sometimes quite personal, the decisions they face are difficult, and they need trusted advisors who can serve as level-headed, experienced sounding-boards.

Developing new business may well take longer—sometimes, caring and empathy for clients is the order of the day, not hard selling.

Principle 1: Get out into the market—actively seek out your clients and try to help them with whatever issues they're facing. Listen, be patient, and be prepared to invest extra time.

Myth: *"I need to cut my prices to attract business."*

Clients would always like a price break, and when they press hard, it's usually because you're perceived as a tradable "expert" and your services are seen as commodities that can be bargained for like salt pork or railroad cars of grain. When times are good, your clients aren't going to pay you more than your standard fees, and when times are bad, you shouldn't discount them either.

What you should be willing to explore, however, are flexible means of payment and delivery. These could include: breaking a large project down into several discrete pieces, which can be decided on and paid for one at a time as the work progresses; agreeing to delay some or all of the invoicing so that it falls into the next fiscal year or budgeting period; conducting a preliminary diagnostic phase of work for a reduced fee, with the explicit understanding that if the benefits are demonstrated, it will lead to a larger phase of full-price work; and offering value-added services as a free "add-on." As a last resort, you may have to reduce your fees or cut your prices, but only do this if you also cut back on what you actually deliver to the client—negotiate what benefits and values are in and which ones are out. Finally, remember that if you grant a client a concession, always ask for one in return.

Principle 2: Don't let clients negotiate your prices downward unless you also negotiate less value (adding more value for the same price is vastly better). If necessary, be willing to propose flexible, creative, and even unorthodox ways of structuring your services and invoicing for them.

Myth: *"Large companies are a safe port during storms."*

Large companies with equally large budgets have historically been the mother lode for a variety of services firms. Their loyalty to service providers and vendors, however, is fleeting. With more centralized control over corporate expenditures than ever before, many Fortune 500 companies now routinely enact across-the-board edicts to reduce operating expenses, leaving outside suppliers high and dry. Furthermore, decision making can become absolutely frozen in these large corporations. The value you add at a small or mid-size company is frequently more clearly recognized. You're often working with higher level executives compared to your interlocutors at a corporate behemoth, and you may also find there is greater loyalty to you as an individual or a firm.

Principle 3: Don't ignore small and medium-size companies, which often have greater flexibility to retain and pay a professional who can really add value.

Myth: *"Now is the time to cut back across the board."*

Indeed, in some areas you will need to monitor and trim your expenditures. But there is one place where, when there is a recession or economic uncertainty, you need to increase investment: marketing and sales. This is an opportunity for the strong to get stronger.

Principle 4: A recession is a good time to increase your market share through enhanced marketing efforts and greater investment in identifying client problems you can solve.

Myth: *"It's more important than ever to demonstrate my specific expertise—it's the only thing clients will pay for when money is tight."*

The slightest discomfort sends most professionals running back to their expert-for-hire bunker. There is some truth to the notion that in good times "generalists" sell well, and in bad times "experts" are more in demand. The real distinction is that *especially* in bad times clients won't buy unless they clearly see the benefits they'll reap, and if you cannot articulate these, you're in for a difficult sale. Remember, expertise is great, but without the ability to create trusted personal relationships, serve as a navigator, and generate real insight for clients, it's worth very little.

Principle 5: In a crisis, insight, judgment, wisdom, and plain level-headedness are often more important than expertise. Experts for hire are commodities in good times and bad.

Myth: *"I need to take any business I can get in times like these."*

The successful professionals I've studied all temper their devotion to clients with great independence, which includes being selective about their clients. Choosing the right clients for your particular services and market focus is one of the most powerful things you can do to shape and grow your business. Don't starve for your principles, but don't panic either, throwing your independence and selectivity out the window.

Executive search professional Susan Bishop, in an article entitled "The Strategic Power of Saying No," describes building her recruiting firm from scratch and the early pressure she felt to take any client she could get.[1] It was only when she learned to focus on the clients who truly matched her strategic focus and strengths—and began saying no to others—that her business truly blossomed.

Principle 6: Accepting any and all business may look good now, but it can eventually drag you down and put you in a potentially worse position when things rebound later on.

Myth: *"I need to spend my time with paying clients."*

We all want to work with winners, but sometimes our clients—like us—are down and out, and that's when they especially need us! I have frequently helped clients who were between jobs. I introduced them to executive recruiters, helped them polish their resumes, and acted as an informal career coach. I didn't do this because I thought there would be some "payback," but when you've lent a hand to someone in need, it is in fact rarely forgotten.

I recall a friend who opened his first ski shop right before a winter with virtually no snow. "I almost went under," he told me, "but a few suppliers supported me and because of them I made it through. I will do business with those companies for the *rest of my life.*"

Remember, too, that if someone loses his job, there is a huge comedown in terms of status and the attention that is lavished on him. Your continuing help and respect will be a breath of fresh air.

Principle 7: A client in need is a client indeed.

Myth: *"It's time to wheel out the tried-and-tested crowd-pleasers— the stuff my clients always used to buy."*

There's nothing wrong with restoring the glitter to tarnished silver or even serving old wine in new bottles. But don't forget that virtually all professional services are knowledge businesses, and the profit in most product businesses comes from knowledge-based services that are sold alongside the product. Former General Electric CEO Jack Welch was no slouch, and he began pushing the growth of General Electric's services years ago. Lou Gerstner, who rescued IBM from near-oblivion in the mid-1990s, did the same thing by building up IBM Global Services; not surprisingly, Sam Palmisano, his successor as CEO, headed that division.

Ask yourself: What new knowledge—insight and wisdom that I will ultimately offer to my clients and embed in my day-to-day work with them—am I going to create this year? This "knowledge" could derive from many different things, including an article that you write, new research that you conduct, a particularly interesting or different piece of client work that you undertake, or a significant course or workshop you attend. At the beginning of each year, leading firms such as McKinsey and Goldman Sachs set up formal R&D budgets aimed at knowledge creation. Why shouldn't you do this as an individual professional?

My coauthor for *Clients for Life,* Professor Jagdish Sheth of the Goizueta Business School at Emory University, is considered a thought-leader in the telecommunications industry. Each year, for example, he delivers a major speech at an industry gathering where he offers a radically new perspective on the evolution of that sector. His audience hungrily debates each year's new idea and looks forward to his latest thinking at the next get-together.

Baltasar Gracián, a sixteenth-century Jesuit priest and advisor to wealthy Spanish nobles, wrote in his book *The Art of Worldly Wisdom,* "You will be esteemed as long as you are new. Novelty pleases everyone because of its variety. . . . A brand new mediocrity is more highly regarded than an extremely talented person to whom we have grown accustomed. When eminences mingle with us they age more quickly."[2] I'm not suggesting that your clients will inevitably dump you and hire the first person who comes along with a new idea, no matter how mediocre he is, just so long as it's "new." But Gracián's observation does highlight a particular aspect of human nature that I think has changed very little in the last 500 years. In other words, you need to bring fresh ideas and perspectives to your clients if you want to keep them engaged over the long term.

Principle 8: Constantly strive to make your old ideas relevant to your clients' current problems, and each year consciously work to develop your next set of frameworks and points of view.

Myth: *"Clients have firm plans and budgets that guide their buying decisions."*

Especially in an uncertain environment, clients often have great difficulty planning and budgeting. They also may feel there is a greater risk associated with taking on an unknown supplier or signing a new contract with a professional they are already doing business with. Here are some things you can do to reduce your client's uncertainty:

- Invest extra time and energy to understand your client's environment and the different ways it may affect his business.
- Guarantee satisfaction with your work. Product-style guarantees are relatively rare in the world of services, but they can achieve the same effect—the reduction of risk and a corresponding increase in trust.
- Offer flexibility in structuring projects and invoicing.
- Shower prospective clients with testimonials and offer twice as many references as they request.
- Set out options and contingency plans that you periodically review together.

Principle 9: Systematically work to reduce your client's uncertainty.

Myth: *"My clients like my work so much they will tell everyone they know about me."*

I blithely believed this myth for years. I always assumed—wrongly—that my most satisfied clients spontaneously gave my name to other business executives every chance they got. I discovered how invalid this assumption was when I asked a couple of my clients for referrals. Their reactions were similar—both were shocked, in a good sense. One said to me, "You always seem so busy—I never dreamed you'd want more business! Of course I'll think of some colleagues I can talk to."

As I outlined in Chapter 5, the final and most often unrealized phase of building your relationship capital comes when your long-standing clients help you to multiply your influence. The most common and direct way of achieving this expansion is by getting referrals. Asking a client for a referral may seem distasteful or embarrassing to you, but if you've done a great job for someone, why wouldn't she be delighted to refer you to someone else? There's a further benefit: When a client publicly states his opinion about you, it reinforces his belief enormously. Typically, in fact, a referee's enthusiasm for you will only grow over time each time he tells another potential client about how much value you've added.

Principle 10: Ask your most loyal clients to recommend you to potential clients.

Myth: *"Publicity is only available to Nobel prize winners and beautiful movie stars."*

Compared to markets of 10 or 20 years ago, those today are more crowded, and third-party endorsements and recognition are more powerful than anything we say about ourselves. So whom would you rather hire: Stockbroker A, who tells you how good he is but you've never heard of him; or Stockbroker B, who also tells you he's great *and* who writes a monthly column on wealth creation for a major newspaper? You may believe you are not newsworthy, but the most absurd things now get people in the media (at the height of last year's holiday shopping season, someone's "10 Worst Toys" list appeared on CNN—and this is *news?*). Think about something you are (or can be) unique at, or a particularly controversial or even off-the-wall perspective that you might write or speak about. Governor Gary Johnson of New Mexico, for example, rocketed overnight from utter obscurity to international celebrity by publicly advocating the decriminalization of drugs. Develop a truly distinctive point of view. You don't have to be as controversial as Governor Johnson, but remember that clients admire boldness, not blandness.

Principle 11: Remember Andy Warhol's observation and get your 15 minutes of fame!

26

Developing Relationships with Foreign Clients

Try Not to Commit These Gaffes

The meeting could not have been more high profile. Sitting at the end of the long, mahogany conference table was the oil minister of Venezuela. His 20 most-senior staff flanked him on both sides. After months of waiting, he was finally going to hear the results of the analysis conducted by a group of prestigious American consultants. All eyes and ears turned to an oversized projection screen on the far wall where the first slide flashed up. "Today," the lead consultant began in heavily accented Spanish, "we are presenting to you Venezuela's first, comprehensive five-year plan for its energy resources."

Unfortunately, the title slide, also written in Spanish, did not say "The Five-Year Plan." It said, "The Five Anuses Plan." The room exploded into hysterical laughter. The consultants became a laughingstock, and the group was never quite able to regain focus on the business issues at hand, especially since "The Five Anuses Plan" was written at the top left of every slide in the package!

This *really* happened to a group of my colleagues 20 years ago. They were in such a rush preparing for their meeting—and so over-confident about their linguistic abilities—that they didn't bother to have a native Spanish speaker proofread their presentation. They knew that when you capitalize a word in Spanish you drop the accent marks (say, over an *E*). But they forgot that *ñ* is a *separate letter of the alphabet* and when capitalized becomes *Ñ*, not *N*—the tilde remains on the top because it's an integral part of the letter, not a separate accent mark. So the word *año*, "year," became the much different and much funnier word *ano*, "anus," to their Venezuelan client.

In your professional career, you may work abroad or have an occasion to deal with clients from another country. Despite the fact that English as a language is more universal than ever, and not withstanding the "homogenization" of cultures around the world, there remain powerful differences in behavior and thinking patterns between different nationalities.

This chapter contains some original and, in some cases, very funny stories I've wanted to tell for some time, but more practically, it sets out some suggestions to help you in developing relationships with non-U.S. clients. Every nationality is different, so think of these as broad principles rather than specific guidelines for individual countries. That said, they are based on practical experience: I lived and worked abroad for 13 years, primarily in England and Italy, but I also spent significant periods of time in countries such as Mexico, Peru, and Japan. I speak four languages, and have done business in 30 countries.

Be Careful with the Language

Shortly after I moved with my family to Rome, my wife went out to a pharmacy to pick up some supplies. A French and psychology major in college, she is quite talented with languages and had already made serious efforts to learn Italian. She walked into the pharmacy and, in her best Italian, asked the white-jacketed young woman behind the counter for "preservative-free contact lens solution." Here is an English translation of what she actually said to the clerk:

"May I have lentil broth without condoms, please?" (I am not kidding.)

The clerk, probably not wishing to embarrass my wife, simply replied, "I'm sorry, we don't carry that."

A stupid mistake? Hysterically funny, yes—stupid, no. I won't dissect the linguistic nuances of this episode, but to give you an example, *preservativo* in Italian means "condom" not "preservative!" This event highlights one of the first pitfalls of being a beginner in a language: Beware of misleading cognates or "false friends." These are words derived from the same root but having unforeseen denotations in one of the two languages.

I'm a strong advocate of learning at least a few words of the language your client speaks. It shows you're interested and willing to invest the time to understand his world. But be very, very careful—it's extraordinarily easy to put your foot in your mouth. Even little expressions that people pick up are usually misused and can come across as insulting or foolish.

For example, in all of the Romance languages and German as well there are important linguistic distinctions between formal and informal usage and titles. There are usually two words for "you" singular (for example, "you" formal and "you" informal), and if you use the wrong one, it is quite a gaffe. I've often heard Americans conveniently adopt the Italian *ciao,* which means both hello and goodbye. In Italy, however, it is normally only used with friends and family. You would never say *ciao* to a client you had just met—it would come across as silly and improper, and it would make you sound like a child.

Not to be outdone by my wife, I committed an equally absurd gaffe—based on a miniscule alteration of pronunciation—with a prospective client a few years later, at a point when I was highly fluent in Italian. In an attempt to convince this potential client to hire my firm, I tried to tell him that after a major project I did with another client, the top executives were "charged up" by the results. Instead, I told him in Italian, "After the project was completed the management team was gassed." He looked at me, appalled, obviously not wishing to hire me and suffer the same fate! The difference was in spelling (and pronouncing) *gasati* versus *gassati*.

The confusion over the word *año* that reduced the meeting with the Venezuelan oil minister to hysterics may seem extreme, but actually it's pretty typical of some people's overconfidence and insensitivity. As a young associate, I was part of a team preparing a not dissimilar presentation to the senior management of a large Mexican company. One of the main themes of the meeting was "allocation of resources." We wrote the slides in Spanish and, like the team in Venezuela, didn't have the document properly reviewed beforehand. We translated "resource allocation" as *alocación de recursos* (sounds pretty similar, so why not?) and that phrase filled the report. We arrived in Mexico City to deliver our presentation, and when the assistant to the CEO reviewed the slides, he was aghast. "Do you know what *alocación de recursos* sounds like in Spanish?" he asked us testily. "It means something like 'driving resources crazy.' " We hung our heads in shame.

By the way, don't think that just because you're in England, where we all theoretically speak the same language, you're going to get away without misunderstandings. A few months after I moved to London, my secretary walked up to my desk and, seeing me struggle to correct a chart I had sketched out in pencil, asked me, "Would you like a rubber?" She meant an *eraser,* of course, not a "condom." Shortly afterward, a female friend who had been part of a luncheon leaned over before departing and said to me, "Well, come knock me up sometime." I turned red, but all she meant was "Come pay me a visit."

Learn to Live with Ambiguity

In American business culture, we're used to clear communications, transparency of operations, and a democratic sharing of information. We like to know where people stand on a transaction, and we want to understand the process being used to reach a decision. In many non-U.S. cultures, however, there is often a great deal of ambiguity that surrounds business dealings. I have found this especially true in Asian and Latin countries, where information is less widely shared and decision making more convoluted.

In America, we are usually told in advance of a meeting who will be there and why they are participating. I can't tell you how many times I have attended business meetings in countries such as Spain, Italy, and Mexico, where twice as many managers as I expected showed up and people mysteriously wandered in and out of the room as the discussions progressed. I once worked for months to set up a meeting with a potential client in France and, when I arrived, discovered that the client had sent, in his place, two executives I had never heard of. I was flustered, but they thought nothing of it.

I remember some U.S. clients being enormously frustrated by a European company to which they were trying to sell a software product. They never got a definitive "yes" or "no" regarding a standards compatibility issue—the manager they were dealing with kept giving them highly ambiguous signals and would never fully share with them the engineering analysis that had been completed.

Does this mean clients from these countries are more devious and Machiavellian than their American counterparts? Absolutely not! A number of factors are usually at work. By not giving a definitive answer to a request, for example, they may be simply trying to keep their options open. These managers may have to contend with more organizational politics than American executives do, and in some cases, they have to deal with more extensive government regulation and interference.

Think Relationship, Not Transaction

Anyone who has worked with businesspeople from countries in Europe, Latin America, and Asia will tell you that they are more relationship-oriented than Americans. Put simply, they want to get to know you as a person before agreeing to do business with you. I was particularly struck by this behavior when I moved back to the United States from Europe in the mid-1990s—everywhere I turned a request for proposal (RFP) appeared and clients didn't seem to have much time or even interest in face-to-face meetings.

Outside the United States, there has always been less financial transparency, and I think that historically people have gravitated toward individuals they knew and trusted, specifically friends and family. Whereas in the United States I might meet just a few times with a potential client before starting some work, I found that in Europe I often had to hold five or more meetings over many months.

This development of trust also depends on where a person grows up. I had a client, for example, who had been raised in a small town in the south of Italy. A wonderful man, he was very traditional and quite suspicious of outsiders, an attitude he no doubt developed while growing up in his remote country village. I met with him every other month for an entire *year* before he became comfortable enough with me to ask me to do a project for his division. The turning point came when he told me, in a state of extreme anxiety, that his eighteen-year-old daughter was going to spend the summer in London, and he was worried sick about her. Having lived for many years in London, I naturally offered to introduce her to some English and American friends there, so that she wouldn't feel totally isolated (this is a small example of going the "extra mile"). After that summer, he hired me as his consultant, and he ended up being extraordinarily loyal to me.

Expect Slower Decision Making

Nowadays, many foreign companies are quick, nimble exemplars of modern management practice. Some, however, still make decisions very slowly. You may have dealings with a state-owned enterprise or a company that has the government as a major shareholder, and the government bureaucracy will inhibit rapid decision making. You may find yourself working with an Asian client, for example, who isn't delegated the authority a typical American manager might enjoy while abroad. You need to be patient and invest extra time to understand how decisions are actually made in the organization you're dealing with.

Recognize Your Own Cultural Biases

Just as we stereotype foreigners, they stereotype Americans. Americans think that the French are arrogant about their food and wine (okay, maybe they are), that Latin Americans don't work as hard (totally false), and that the Japanese aren't creative (hey, the people who invented tube hotels and Pokeman can't be that stodgy). Americans are, depending on whom you talk to, loud, obnoxious, too familiar, boorish, culturally ignorant, lousy cooks, right-wing, and politically naïve.

When you work with clients from other countries, try to recognize the biases you may implicitly be acting on. At the same time, be more *neutral* in your own behavior, and try to listen more and talk less. I'll never forget sitting in a famous restaurant along the Via Veneto in Rome, having lunch with the chairman of a U.S. company. He was an extraordinarily intelligent, kind, and thoughtful man. But after being served a cappuccino, he waved to the waiter and shouted quite loudly, "You know, the one thing you guys just don't know how to make in this country is a good cup of coffee!" I wanted to crawl out of my skin and hide under the table. The waiter just smiled and waved back. Thankfully, he didn't speak a word of English.

To succeed in working with non-U.S. clients, you've got to accept greater ambiguity and uncertainty, be patient with the decision-making process, and invest in building a relationship before you win a transaction. It helps to learn some of their language, but tread carefully as you try out your newfound vocabulary—you may end up ordering something in a restaurant that you won't be able to eat. Listen more and talk less as you tone down your own chauvinism.

Come to think of it, these aren't bad practices for building better relationships at home.

27

Becoming a Firm That Makes Rain

How Great Organizations Build Clients for Life

Some organizations seem to draw clients in and keep them by means of some powerful gravitational pull. Showing exemplary internal teamwork, they serve their clients' needs reliably and confidently. Others—and I've encountered more than a few—struggle with client defections. When there's a sale, everyone bickers about who should get the credit. When something goes wrong, they quickly point fingers. What makes the difference?

Many of the principles guiding you as an *individual* professional to develop client loyalty can be applied to *firmwide* or *institutional* strategies for making rain on a regular basis with clients.

There are seven areas that your organization can focus on to enhance its rain-making abilities with existing clients: professional development, relationship management, knowledge creation, compensation and rewards, client service, trust, and culture. Overlooking any one of them is likely to bring on a client-threatening drought.

Slogans don't make you a client-focused organization—you reach this goal by implementing many small things and having senior management set a clear example. If you want to become a firm that consistently makes rain by building long-term client loyalty, look hard at your policies and practices in each of the following seven areas.

1. Professional Development

As you might expect, in their training and development programs, most organizations focus on teaching technical skills and core professional competencies. Training on "softer" topics such as client relationship management, however, is often absent. There are two primary reasons for this oversight: First, many managers assume this is an intuitive skill that cannot be taught; second, until recently there haven't been any established curricula that effectively do teach it.

The hierarchy of developmental needs for any business professional includes:

- Core competencies of the profession—for example, legal skills for a lawyer, selling skills for a salesperson; systems integration knowledge for an IT consultant.
- Product knowledge.
- Industry knowledge.
- Management and leadership skills.
- Client relationship-building skills.

Some firms that I have worked with or observed are doing several things to enhance their professional development efforts around the last item on this list. A major accounting firm, for example, has developed a "business advisor" program for all of its partners. Drawing on the principles in my first book, *Clients for Life,* as well as other sources, this firm's business advisor program focuses on teaching client listening, big-picture thinking, trust building, and the other core attributes of client advisors.

In addition, a large consulting firm created for its consultants a similar training program called "The Influential Advisor." It is a comprehensive learning experience divided into five two-day modules that begin with "establishing trust and credibility" and end with "adding continuous value." At its center is a complex client case that slowly develops its various facets during the five modules. A variety of tools are available to the course participants: information about consulting methodologies, short videos on different aspects of relationship-building, an archive of tips and suggestions from more experienced consultants.

I would encourage you to look broadly at your company's professional development efforts, and ask whether they include these relationship-oriented skills that are becoming increasingly important. For instance, in his book *Emotional Intelligence,* Daniel Goleman says that most studies of executive performance show that two-thirds of success is due to emotional intelligence factors—interpersonal skills, empathy, optimism, motivation, the ability to communicate—whereas only one-third is based on intellectual skills.[1] Historically we have tended to emphasize the latter, while ignoring the former.

2. Relationship Management

The more products and services that you offer to your clients, the more difficult becomes the task of relationship management. Banks faced this dilemma years ago, as financial services products proliferated in the 1970s and 1980s. A financial institution might have 10 or 20 distinct products or services, each marketed to the same client base. So how do you coordinate this set of offerings?

There are three distinct dimensions to relationship management that you need to think about: assignment of a relationship manager, account development, and institutionalized listening.

First, should one person be responsible for the overall relationship? Many companies are moving toward this solution, especially for their largest and most important clients. At the consulting firm Hewitt Associates, for example, a senior level managing consultant (MC) is responsible for each major client relationship. The MC becomes that client's trusted advisor for all of its human resources needs. The MC coordinates the marketing and delivery of a variety of Hewitt services, from consulting to benefits outsourcing, and he or she meets frequently with client executives to explore their needs and ensure that Hewitt is delivering on its promises.

A relationship manager is expensive and doesn't always make sense. If the buyers for your services within the client's organization are completely different, then coordination may not be worth the cost. If it's a relatively small client, then spending a lot of resources on high-level relationship management also isn't worthwhile.

Second, relationship management has to include a client or account development process. This is different from account "planning," which is often a dry exercise conducted at the beginning of the fiscal year and which typically suffers from lack of follow-up. The client development process, in contrast, is a highly effective discipline that very few companies implement, and it can have an important impact on the breadth and richness of the relationship.

Here is a very simple process that you can follow for your top-tier clients: Twice a year, organize a two- or three-hour account development session. It should include staff who are working on the client relationship; a facilitator (who can be the relationship or assignment leader); and at least one senior-level executive or professional who is not involved in the client relationship at all. I recommend preparation of a background package of five or six slides to include client background, a history of your business with the client, key industry trends, strategic and operational issues facing the company, organizational structure and key decision makers, and possible further areas for collaboration. The facilitator leads the group through this information, with a focus on idea generation: "Are we dealing with the right level of executive? Who else in the company should be part of the network? What other needs does this client have that we could fulfill? Could we partner with this client to add value in new ways?" The end result should be a list of action steps aimed at better serving the client; deepening the relationship; and pursuing specific opportunities for expansion that have been identified.

The third dimension of relationship management is institutionalized listening, which I discussed at the start of Chapter 15. This can be done on several different levels. Hewitt Associates surveys several hundred of its clients each year, distributing a comprehensive questionnaire that covers everything from client satisfaction to the client's perception of the skills of Hewitt's lead consultants. On another level, the leading law firm of Fulbright & Jaworski has developed a program of "chairman's visits." Each year, its chairman personally visits its top twenty clients. These are not just lunch-and-golf sessions but substantive exchanges about the client's emerging needs and satisfaction with Fulbright's legal services.

Clients rarely tell you in advance that they are going to leave. Usually, they just stop doing business with you, or the amount of business slowly declines over time. Only by institutionalizing your ability to listen and tune in can you prevent a small dissatisfaction or misunderstanding from turning into a client defection. On the positive side, this type of multifaceted listening will allow you to become aware of client needs that previously escaped your notice.

3. Knowledge Creation

A Boston management consulting firm called Emergence Consulting, which specializes in growth strategies, works with a small group of leading academics who have developed several breakthrough concepts in the area of strategic innovation. What's unique about Emergence is that it has institutionalized the development of intellectual capital—of knowledge creation and dissemination—by organizing itself around key idea areas. It has, for example, assigned a permanent project manager to work with each academic in his or her area of focus. This person helps to develop and codify the theory, create practical ways to implement it in business organizations, and train other consultants. Francis Gouillart, Emergence's founder, describes this institutionalization of knowledge creation: "We've essentially organized the firm around several powerful concepts of strategy and innovation, and then created formal roles to manage them from theory to delivery."

On a different scale, consulting giant McKinsey has fostered an entire culture around the concept of knowledge creation. Every year each industry sector or practice head is charged with developing a "knowledge creation agenda" for his or her business, and individual consultants are evaluated on their yearly contribution to knowledge development.

Why is institutionalized knowledge creation—and its ultimate transfer to clients—so important? As mentioned previously, most basic products and services, from telephone switches to legal contracts, are commodities: Many suppliers provide them. What distinguishes you are those fresh ideas about your client's business and industry and insights into how your product or service can help solve problems and enable your client to meet his goals.

But there's an additional reason, which is more subtle: Like all of us, clients are enamored of hot ideas and hot products. As Baltasar Gracián wrote 500 years ago, "Novelty pleases everyone." You need to continually bring fresh ideas and perspectives to your relationships or else you risk being supplanted by "brand-new mediocrities."

Most corporations have formal R&D budgets, but many professional service firms, oddly, do not. They assume innovation and idea development happen naturally during the course of client assignments. To avoid the inevitable spiral of commoditization, you need to think about creating a formal R&D or innovation budget within your organization. Each year, you might fund promising research efforts focused on industry trends, competitive developments, or the policies and practices of leading executives who are your clients. The results can be channeled into speeches, books, articles, seminars, and a host of other marketing activities that create opportunities to get in front of key client executives.

These efforts will inform your current services and fuel the development of new offerings. They also increase the prestige of your company. The polling firm Gallup, for example, created an entire consulting practice off the back of its book *First, Break All the Rules.* Advertising great David Ogilvy's brilliant book, *Ogilvy on Advertising,* is still widely read by executives both inside and outside that industry.

"This is really going to give us visibility with our CEO prospects."

4. Compensation and Rewards

As you will recall, the "rainmaker" I described in the Introduction grossly exaggerated the magnitude of a client sale right around bonus time. If compensation is overly focused on sales or business origination, the results can be tragic: a culture develops in which revenue rules over quality and service, and the only news you receive about sales and marketing efforts is filtered and positive.

Ultimately, revenue should be a measure of client satisfaction, but in the short run, even this relationship can get distorted. One company I knew had a powerful selling process but poor delivery of its services. Its revenues grew tremendously over several years, but mostly because the company moved from client to client, deploying its nearly unstoppable new business development "machine" to great effect.

Egon Zehnder International (EZI), a large executive search firm, presents an interesting counterpoint to the traditional wisdom that you must single-mindedly reward individuals for revenue growth. Its founder, Egon Zehnder, says this about compensation: "Today, most consulting firms, law firms, and so forth consider seniority irrelevant—and occasionally something much worse. They believe pay should be based on performance and, more specifically, individual performance. That's why at most professional firms, people are paid according to the size of their client billings and how good they are at bringing in new clients."[2] Many EZI clients are multinational corporations, and cooperation between its various offices around the world is paramount to conducting successful searches. EZI has grown in revenue and profits every year for the last 37 years, and has a partner turnover rate of 2 percent, which is a fraction of the industry average. How does it pay its partners to achieve these results? As Zehnder explains, "We prefer to stick with the old-fashioned way to pay. In addition to base salaries, the firm gives partners equal shares of the profit and another set of profit shares that are adjusted only for length of tenure as a partner. There is no formal procedure for tracking the performance of country offices, let alone individuals." Rewarding seniority seems like an antiquated concept, yet in this business, the longer your tenure, the broader your network of executives, the deeper your knowledge of hundreds of organizations, and the more continuity you have with long-term clients.

I'm not advocating that EZI's approach is right for every organization, but it certainly gives us food for thought. Some would argue that EZI's compensation system might not, at least in theory, sufficiently motivate individual professionals, especially younger ones with less tenure. Clearly, though, it has developed a culture of achievement that is fueled by individual self-motivation and a group ethos oriented toward marketplace success. In most businesses, internal teamwork is essential to serving clients' interests, and in EZI's case, this aspect is especially emphasized by the compensation system. The point is that a company's rewards system needs to take into account much more than just individual revenue production.

The timing of revenue inflows should also be part of the equation. I know a few firms, for example, which based incentive compensation not just on the initial sale but also on the residual revenues for years afterwards. In a similar vein, Siebel Systems bases most of its incentive compensation for its salespeople on customer satisfaction scores at least four quarters after the sale.

5. Client Service

Jeff Klopf is the general counsel for Security Capital Corporation, one of the country's largest property companies that was recently purchased by GE Capital. Over the years, Klopf has used many of the largest law and accounting firms in the country to advise on Security Capital's frequent M&A and corporate finance transactions. In speaking of client service, he says, "As far as the basic legal work goes, there are many firms that can do a good job. A few, though, really distinguish themselves through extraordinary client service. For example, the partners at one firm I deal with are *always* reachable and available to me. I never get voice mail, which has become irritating not least because I never know when someone is going to listen to my message. Instead, my call is forwarded through to another office where they're working or to their cell phones. Or, I speak to their assistant who is always completely knowledgeable about the issues we're working on. In contrast, I called a firm last week and left three messages—a day later I still had no reply! That's completely unacceptable."

Client service can include many different dimensions:

- Availability of key professionals.
- Knowledgeable support staff who are entirely familiar with each client assignment and know the client by name.

- Rapid resolution of administrative questions or glitches involving things such as invoicing.
- Your ability to respond rapidly to client requests and inquiries.

Client service will mean different things to different clients. The best way to find out what's important is to ask your clients what really matters to them and what standards they expect from you.

6. Trust

Just as individual professionals need to build trust with clients, so does the institution as a whole. There are a number of things you can do at the firm level to create a "trusted brand." These include:

- *Ensure consistent quality of staff.* If every person a client encounters from your organization meets the highest quality standards and does great work—be they a professional, manager, or a member of the administrative staff—then individual trust will be transformed into institutional trust. This works internally, as well. If I work in the Chicago office of a large company but have doubts about the caliber of my counterpart in San Francisco, then I'll hesitate to involve him in my client relationship, even if he brings badly needed skills to the table. Any company-wide approach to relationship management will fail if this type of trust between colleagues is not consistently strong. Some of the best professional firms I know actually turn away a qualified candidate out of fear that they may hire a person who is not right for the job. They believe that the actual cost of the latter is greater than the opportunity cost of the former.
- *Offer service guarantees.* As mentioned in Chapter 4, these guarantees are a way of reducing risk and building trust. It's important for a client to know that the individual he is working with will always come through for him. If in addition

there is some form of firm-sponsored assurance, the effect is even more powerful.

- *Only undertake business you can successfully deliver.* In a manufacturing business, customers will still tolerate (or are forced to put up with!) a certain number of defects. In service businesses, in contrast, there is almost zero tolerance of less-than-perfect work. During the dot-com mania in the late 1990s, many service firms undertook assignments in areas where they lacked real capability. The result was, ultimately, tainted reputations and clients who were burned.
- *Cultivate positive associations.* If we perceive that an individual associates with people we respect, we are more likely to feel positively about him or her. For example, if a financial advisor we meet manages the investments for the mayor of our hometown, we are automatically predisposed to like her (assuming we respect the mayor). I believe the same effect works at the firm level: To the extent you work with well-respected clients and have prestigious business partners, there will be a stronger halo of institutional trust around your organization. This is why, for example, you will see small technology companies advertising their partnerships with organizations such as Microsoft, General Electric, and Cisco.
- *Rigorously uphold the highest ethical and professional standards.* By systematically cultivating a culture of high ethical standards—and communicating your policies to clients—you will greatly increase clients' trust in your entire organization. After the debacle at Enron, many clients are looking for explicit assurance that their interests are consistently put first.

7. Culture

In every organization, a set of implicit beliefs and values guides daily behavior. A client-focused culture will help ensure that decisions are consistently made in favor of actions that add value, build trust, and go the extra mile for clients. To a great extent, your organization's culture will be driven by all of the factors discussed here—the rewards structure, relationship management, client service standards, and so on. At the top of my list is also the behavior of top management, which, after all, sets the example for everyone else. I have worked with some firms where the managing directors or partners actually spend very little time with clients. They delegate most of the delivery work, and focus on setting and monitoring internal policies and procedures, generally by holding interminable internal meetings. In contrast, I recall a discussion with Orit Gadiesh, the chairman of consultants Bain & Company. A well-respected CEO advisor, Gadiesh told me, "I spend 70 percent of my time with our major clients."

An exemplar of a CEO who has created this type of client-centered culture is Tom Siebel of Siebel Systems. Siebel Systems sells complex customer relationship management software to corporations around the world, and Siebel has systematically built an organization to sell and service this software that is itself completely customer-centric. In an interview published in the *Harvard Business Review,* Siebel said, "If we have to choose between dealing with a customer satisfaction issue or developing a product, we deal with the customer first. If we have to choose between pursuing a new sales opportunity or dealing with customer satisfaction, we deal with the customer first. At every fork in the road, it's 'customer first.' And it always pays off."[3]

Early in the company's development, Siebel was offered a huge contract with MCI, which at the time was a small customer. He concluded that because Siebel Systems did not have the resources to ramp up its MCI business *and* service other customers, he had to decline the contract. Eventually, despite being turned down for the order—or perhaps because of it—MCI became one of Siebel System's biggest accounts. In another telling example, when a major Siebel Systems installation at Sun Microsystems was not working well, Siebel sent in a team of engineers to fix it. They worked in

24-hour shifts, seven days a week, until it was working properly. Siebel says, "As it turned out, the problem didn't have anything to do with our software, but we didn't point fingers at the other vendor and say, 'The problem is with you guys.' Our approach was to solve Sun's problem and get the system live."[4]

In designing and facilitating offsite strategic planning retreats with my clients, I always recommend including, in some way, the voice of their customers. Sometimes I'll organize a panel of customers or clients to attend the session, or have them call in to be interviewed while the entire executive group listens to the feedback. It's always illuminating.

Becoming a Firm That Makes Rain

Organizations that build strong loyalty with clients are often also good at building internal loyalty. After all, the same factors that instill client loyalty—value-added, trust, and the extra mile—motivate employees to stay with your company. Employees have to feel that their company is adding-value by giving them interesting work today and helping them build the skills for a successful career in the future; that their colleagues and top management have integrity and can be trusted; and that the company will go the extra mile for *them* if they have a personal or professional issue to grapple with.

Are You Sustaining Your Relationships Year after Year?

✔ Do you regularly stay in touch with past clients, keeping abreast of their work and careers?

✔ Do your clients provide you with referrals and leverage *their* network to disseminate your reputation and ideas?

✔ Do you treat every long-standing client like a brand-new client? Do you bring to each meeting the same freshness, enthusiasm, and new ideas that you were able to offer when you first started the relationship?

✔ Have you become partners with any of your clients in ways that extend beyond the normal buyer-seller relationship?

✔ Do you bring information or insights to your clients that are unique or proprietary?

✔ Have you cultivated an attitude of independent wealth, or do you have a scarcity outlook?

✔ When dealing with foreign clients, do you expect the same speed of decision-making and organizational clarity that you're used to at home? Or do you consciously take into account cultural differences and invest the extra time that may be required to form a relationship?

✔ Do all elements of your company's organization, systems, and processes—professional development, rewards, relationship management, R&D, and so on—support the development of long-term client relationships?

PART FOUR

GETTING STARTED: A SELF-ASSESSMENT

28

Do You Have the Ability to Make Rain?

Two Assessment Tools for Individuals and Organizations

In this book, you've been exposed to many different ideas and strategies that can help you build long-term client loyalty. So where do you start? I suggest that you begin by evaluating your existing client relationships, and then assessing your and your firm's ability to make rain.

First, evaluate what role you're really playing with your clients. For each of your clients, are you an expert for hire, a steady supplier, or a trusted advisor? Don't worry—very few professionals can honestly say that they are a trusted advisor to *all* their clients. It's quite natural that some relationships will fall into each of these three categories. The point is to recognize where you stand, understand why, and then develop strategies to move to the next level. It's also useful to think about those relationships where you really are part of the inner circle: What's the secret to your success with these particular clients?

Next, you need to inventory your own skills and, if you work with an organization, your company's ability to create long-term client loyalty. Working with a leading authority in the area of assessment design, I have developed two separate assessment tools to help you do this. Both, at this writing, will be available free for one year after publication. The first is focused on you as an *individual professional;* the second, on your *company.* The assessments themselves are located on my Web site, which is www.andrewsobel.com. When you go to the site, you will see clear instructions on the home page for accessing the *Making Rain* assessment tools. A series of prompts will lead you through each questionnaire, and your score will be automatically calculated. The tests themselves will be a valuable review, because they systematically go through many of the key learning points in this book.

These assessments will take you through all of the major facets of relationship-building and loyalty creation, that I'll briefly summarize here.

The Self-Assessment

The self-assessment asks you to evaluate yourself and your client relationships along a number of dimensions, including:

- *Personal attributes.* This section of the assessment focuses on the core attributes of successful client advisors, which are the principal subject of my book *Clients for Life.* It covers things such as empathy, selfless independence, big-picture thinking, judgment, and other characteristics.
- *Trust-building.* This section addresses the elements of the trust formula, such as integrity, competence, and intimacy, and all of the strategies that contribute to likability.
- *Relationship strategies.* Here, you'll be asked to assess your competence and understanding of a variety of tools, techniques,

and strategies that help build and develop long-term relationships. These include the client loyalty equation, the use of breakthrough strategies, relationship capital, migration paths, and so on.

- *Relationship philosophy and attitudes.* The professionals I have studied who keep their clients for life have very distinct attitudes and outlooks, including focus on clients' hidden creases, use indirect methods, exercise a doubting mind, employ a mission orientation, and have an abundance outlook.
- *Client behaviors.* The ultimate test of whether or not you build lifelong client loyalty is actual client behavior. In this part of the assessment, you'll be asked to describe the nature of your client relationships along several important dimensions.

The Company Assessment

The company assessment asks you to evaluate different facets of your organization's strategy, structure, processes, and culture that combine to *institutionalize* the ability to make rain and build long-term loyalty. These points are consistent with the framework I set out in Chapter 27:

- *Professional development.* Do your firm's learning and development programs—and career management practices—address the core competencies needed to build and manage long-term relationships?
- *Trust building.* Does your organization engage in practices that create an institutional brand that clients trust?
- *Relationship Management.* Does your firm employ multiple strategies to ensure comprehensive management of key client relationships, including institutionalized client listening, formal relationship management structures, account development, and management of your client base as a portfolio?
- *Client service.* Client-centered companies that consistently make rain demonstrate extraordinarily high levels of client

service along several dimensions. This section assesses your practices and capacity for great client service.

- *Rewards.* To what extent does your reward system motivate the behaviors that are necessary for long-term relationship building?
- *Culture.* Does senior management and your colleagues exemplify values and principles that support client-centered behavior?
- *Knowledge creation.* Does the organization have any formal processes to create new ideas, concepts, and approaches for clients?
- *Client behaviors.* In this section, you'll be asked questions about your firm's client base that will provide a "check" to your answers in the first seven areas.

These assessment tools will provide you with an excellent sense of your strengths and weaknesses. Ultimately, you will be able to compare your own assessment with those of other professionals.

The practices that build client loyalty—adding value, building trust, and going the extra mile—take time to implement. Relationships, by their very nature, require patience and hard work to develop. Remember that you've got many assets you can leverage, including your existing relationship capital—especially your past and present client relationships—as well as your professional skills and experience.

In thinking about the process of building long-term relationships, I'm reminded of a story told about the great French Marshal and statesman, Louis Hubert Lyautey. He once asked his gardener to plant a tree in his garden. The gardner objected, telling Lyautey that this particular type of tree would take nearly 100 years to reach maturity. "In that case," the Marshal responded, "there is no time to lose. Plant it this afternoon."

So don't procrastinate or get discouraged. Start now and begin to apply, day-by-day, these ideas and strategies to your own client relationships.

A Pantheon of
Client Advisors

Throughout history, great leaders have availed themselves of trusted counselors drawn from a variety of professions and disciplines. This section profiles a number of these historic advisors, some of whom have had an enormous impact on the outcome of major events such as World War II. The art of advising has been around for thousands of years, and we can learn a lot from those who went before us.

The Oracle at Delphi (about 600 B.C. to 362 A.D.), Greece, was located in the temple of Apollo which was a pilgrimage for leaders throughout the ancient world for nearly 1000 years. The actual oracle was a woman, called the Pythia, who would chew laurel leaves prior to each consultation, and then, in a delirium, mumble her answer. When King Croesus asked the Pythia if he should attack Persia, she responded, "If you attack, a great empire will fall." Unfortunately, he forgot to ask *which* empire, and he was roundly defeated by the Persians.

Aristotle (384–322 B.C.) acquired a breadth of knowledge that is probably unrivaled in intellectual history. He was a great scholar and philosopher but also an advisor to influential Greeks and Macedonians. He wrote over 50 books, with titles such as *On the Soul, On Pleasure, On the Sciences, On Magnets,* and *Proverbs,* and introduced the revolutionary concept of bodies of knowledge, which is a cornerstone of our modern educational system. His most famous student and advisee was Alexander the Great, whom Aristotle tutored for three years while he was an adolescent.

Merlin (450–536 A.D.), according to some historians, was a real person, although clearly the Arthurian legends are a blend of both fact and fiction. A Welsh religious figure, Merlin advised not just King Arthur but his father, Uther, and several other monarchs as well. It was reputedly Merlin who counseled Uther to establish the Knights of the Round Table, and he foretold that Uther's true heir would be revealed by a test that involved drawing a sword from a stone. Legend holds that Merlin raised Arthur in the forest, educating him and preparing him for his eventual role as king.

Leonardo da Vinci (1452–1519) became one of the greatest artists and most inventive minds in history with virtually no formal education. An elegant dresser who had impeccable posture, Leonardo cut a striking figure as he strolled around Renaissance Florence. Like Aristotle before him and Benjamin Franklin after, he was a perpetual learner whose curiosity was never sated. He had a doubting mind that never accepted that the way things were done was necessarily the best or right way. Although most of his extraordinary inventions were never built during his lifetime, a handful of his paintings, such as the Mona Lisa, survive today, and they are considered among the masterworks of Western culture.

Niccolò Machiavelli (1469–1527) was in many ways the precursor to Tom Peters and other twentieth-century business book authors. His book, *The Prince,* sets out the principles for great leadership, just as Peter's *In Search of Excellence* tried to codify the characteristics of successful companies (arguably, *The Prince* has stood the test of time a bit better than the Peter's book). A diplomat, brilliant thinker, and superb writer, Machiavelli has to some extent been unfairly criticized over the centuries for advocating corrupt leadership practices in *The Prince*. This view is far too narrow, and there has recently been a resurgence of interest in his writing over the past 10 years.

Thomas More (1478–1535) was a brilliant lawyer who, because of his impeccable judgment and rock-solid integrity, was drawn into

Henry VIII's inner circle of advisors, eventually becoming lord chancellor. More was an example of "heroic" *selfless independence*—he was devoted to his client, the king, but also independent from him, and unwilling to compromise his most dearly-held principles and religious beliefs. More was immortalized twice—first by the Catholic Church, which bestowed sainthood on him, and second by Robert Bolt's play *A Man for all Seasons,* which chronicled his rise and fall and was made into a major motion picture. Peter Ackroyd's 1999 biography of More, *The Life of Thomas More,* is a marvelous evocation of that period in history.

Iñigo de Oñaz y Loyola (1491–1556), the founder of the Jesuits, was a troubled youth who had more than one run-in with the law in his early years. As an adult, he underwent a spiritual awakening, and subsequently created an organization that has endured for nearly 500 years. Loyola insisted on a deep, broad education for his followers, and Jesuit schools have educated millions over the centuries. The Jesuits, who are trained to be able to expertly undertake any task, anywhere, are exemplars of the deep generalist that succeeds so well in business today.

Baltasar Gracián (1601–1658) was born in Aragon, Spain. Gracián became a Jesuit priest, senior church administrator, and advisor to many famous Spaniards. He was known for his clever aphorisms, many of which are found in his delightful book *The Oracle,* which is full of wisdom and insight about human nature. Throughout their history, the Jesuits have exercised enormous influence as advisors to business and political leaders; today, consultants McKinsey & Company have sometimes been compared to the Jesuits in terms of their influence on corporate CEOs.

Benjamin Franklin (1706–1790) is in many ways America's answer to the multitalented Leonardo da Vinci. There is hardly a sphere that Franklin did not contribute to, including politics, literature, science, government, and others. An avid inventor, the free-standing stove he designed survives even today in modern form, and his early experiments with electricity placed him at the forefront of the scientific investigators of his time. He developed his "indirect" method early on, using humor and gentle prodding rather than direct criticism or disagreement as a means of influencing others. He was a master at building relationship capital, making many friends and few enemies despite his enormous successes. Franklin's autobiography, full of self-improvement maxims, could easily be considered a harbinger of today's self-help books that populate the bestseller lists.

Mayer Amschel Rothschild (and family) (1744–1812) started out selling antique coins, but in short order was able to parlay his relationships with wealthy German aristocrats into a banking business. His five sons ran merchant banking operations in five major European financial centers, and together constituted the first true multinational bank. They were able to consistently underbid their rivals as well as offer banking services that few if any competitors had the scale and capability to match. The Rothschilds were masters as cultivating relationships with a variety of government officials, high and low, and they developed their own unique sources of information about the financial markets in which they operated. In the early nineteenth century, they were the wealthiest family in the world, and their capital resources exceeded those of the Bank of France.

John Pierpont Morgan (1837–1913) was the first relationship banker. He wasn't content to simply lend money to his clients—he wanted to become their chief advisor, confessor, and, ultimately, shareholder. Morgan was driven by an intense need for order and stability more than power, money, or even the desire to run a large bank. Many of his business investments were based on his desire to create order in chaotic markets like railroads and steel. Business and political leaders of all kinds sought him out for advice, and he relished the role. He was an excellent listener, and would often let others go on for hours before interjecting his opinion or trying to steer the outcome a certain way. *The House of Morgan* by Ron Chernow and *Morgan: American Financier* by Jean Strouse, are excellent books about J. P. Morgan and his bank.

Gertrude Bell (1868–1926) is one of the few female historical advisors about which good documentation exists. The daughter of a wealthy English industrialist, Bell was one of the first women to attend Oxford, and shortly after graduating she set off for an extended journey through the Middle Eastern. She had an uncanny knack for being quickly accepted by the various Middle Eastern cultures and her keen intelligence, objectivity, and great listening skills made her a sought-after advisor by both Western and Arab leaders. Toward the end of her life, she became the most important personal advisor to King Faisal, the first ruler of modern Iraq. *Desert Queen,* by Janet Wallach, is a colorful account of Bell's remarkable life.

George Marshall (1880–1959) was a mediocre student in high school, but once he enrolled in the Virginia Military Institute, he began to shine. He was a man of enormous integrity and conviction, and he always spoke his mind, even in the face of overwhelming authority. He was one of the few individuals in the military who was willing to stand up to Franklin Roosevelt, a quality which led the powerful president to pull Marshall into his inner circle. After leading the Allied armies to victory in World War II, he designed and implemented the Marshall Plan to rebuild Europe. A key advisor to both Roosevelt and Truman, he became Truman's secretary of state in 1947 and secretary of defense in 1950. Marshall was awarded the Nobel Peace Prize in 1953.

Harry Hopkins (1890–1946), who was trained as a social worker, worked for Franklin Roosevelt while he was governor of New York. When Roosevelt became president, he quickly called on Hopkins—someone he had learned to respect and trust unconditionally—and brought him into his administration. Hopkins lacked any kind of experience in politics and economic affairs, but he was a versatile problem solver, and he never lost sight of the president's agenda. Other world leaders also developed great confidence in Hopkins, and they respected his capacity to translate Roosevelt's objectives into realizable plans and specific actions. Roosevelt sent Hopkins to visit Churchill during the blitz, and Hopkins became instrumental in convincing Roosevelt—and eventually the whole country—that Britain desperately needed U.S. support against Hitler. Hopkins had fatal intestinal ailment that halted his political ambitions but which increased his influence and power as an advisor.

Peter Drucker (1909–   ), alive and well, can fairly be called "historic" in the sense that he is already a leading if not *the* leading figure in the history of modern management philosophy and practice.

Today, he sometimes refers to himself as an "insultant" rather than a consultant—a reference to the difficult, prickly questions he asks his clients. Drucker is a key advisor to leaders in the nonprofit sector, and continue to write articles and books even though he is in his early 90s.

David Ogilvy (1911–1999) practiced a number of trades—apprentice chef, stove salesman, farmer, and British intelligence agent—before entering the advertising profession. He then went on to become one of the greatest advertising geniuses of all time. Ogilvy was a true deep generalist—multicultural in outlook and widely read, he worked with the famous pollster George Gallup for several years in the United States, learning about emerging quantitative market research techniques. Ogilvy wrote several witty, clever books (such as *Ogilvy on Advertising*) and was always full of irreverent advice (such as "you should fire one major client every year"). He is best remembered today for his establishment of the importance of branding.

Henry Kissinger (1923–   ) is a brilliant big-picture thinker—he truly epitomized the advisor who is able to pull vast amounts of information together into a coherent whole, see the patterns, and draw relevant conclusions. As advisor to two U.S. presidents, Richard Nixon and Gerald Ford, during the Vietnam and Cold War eras, Kissinger was frequently torn between looking after the interests of his presidential clients and enhancing his own prestige. Walter Issacson's biography, *Kissinger,* is an entertaining read that chronicles the bizarre relationship between Kissinger and his main client, President Richard Nixon.

Notes

Introduction: Learning to Make Rain All of the Time

1. Ford Harding, *Rain Making: The Professional's Guide to Attracting New Clients* (Holbrook, MA: Bob Adams, 1994).

Chapter 1: The Loyalty Equation: Three Factors That Determine Your Client's Loyalty

1. Frederick F. Reichheld, *Loyalty Rules! How Today's Leaders Build Lasting Relationships* (Boston: Harvard Business School Press, 2001).
2. Robert Cialdini, *Influence: The Psychology of Persuasion* (New York: William Morrow, 1984).
3. Niccolò Machiavelli, *The Prince,* trans. George Bull (London: Penguin Books, 1995), p. 1.

Chapter 2: Are You an Extraordinary Advisor?

1. This framework of seven attributes is drawn from Jagdish Sheth and Andrew Sobel, *Clients for Life: Evolving from an Expert for Hire to an Extraordinary Advisor* (New York: Simon & Schuster, 2000).
2. These techniques are discussed in detail in Chapter 5 of *Clients for Life,* "The Big Picture: Cultivating Powers of Synthesis."

Chapter 3: Breakthrough Strategies for Experts

1. John Grisham, *The Firm* (New York: Random House, 1991), p. 7.

Chapter 6: Benjamin Franklin's Secret Weapon

1. H. W. Brands, *The First American* (New York: Doubleday, 2000), p. 3.
2. Ibid.
3. Ibid., p. 166.
4. Ibid., p. 167.

Chapter 7: Why a Client Might Like You

1. Jane Austen, *Selected Letters* 1796–1817 R. W. Chapman, Editor (Oxford: Oxford University Press, 1955), p. 19.
2. Dale Carnegie, *How to Win Friends and Influence People* (New York: Pocket Books, 1936).
3. Robert B. Cialdini, *Influence: The Psychology of Persuasion* (New York: William Morrow, 1984).
4. Ibid., p. 173.
5. "Flattering Classes," *Daily Mail Associated Newspapers* (April 26, 2002, p. 23). Professor Roos Vonk of the University of Holland, after a trial involving 300 volunteers, states that "It's in superficial relationships, especially with others at work, that flattery is most powerful."
6. Carnegie, p. 4.
7. Cialdini, p. 174.

Chapter 9: Leonardo da Vinci: Why Lutes and Madonnas Matter

1. Serge Bramly, *Leonardo: The Artist and the Man* (London: Penguin Books, 1992), p. 173.
2. Ibid., p. 187.
3. Ibid., p. 323.
4. Ibid., p. 267.

Chapter 10: Finding the Hidden Creases: Influencing Your Clients

1. Kenneth Kushner, *One Arrow, One Life* (Boston: Charles E. Tuttle: 2000), p. 62.
2. http://www.cp-tel.net/miller/BilLee/quotes/Franklin.html.
3. Gary A. Williams and Robert B. Miller, "Change the Way You Persuade," *Harvard Business Review,* May, 2002, p. 65.
4. Robert and Dorothy Grover Bolton, *Social Style/Management Style: Developing Productive Work Relationships* (New York: AMACOM, 1984).
5. Elements of this framework are adapted from Lynne C. Lancaster and David Stillman, *When Generations Collide: Who They Are, Why They Clash, How to Solve the Generational Puzzle at Work* (New York: Harper Business, 2002), and Bruce Tulgan, *Managing Generation X: How to Bring Out the Best in Young Talent* (Santa Monica, CA: Merrit Publishing, 1995).

Chapter 12: The Relationship Masters

1. Malachi Martin, *The Jesuits* (New York: Simon & Schuster, 1987), p. 177.

Chapter 13: The Doubting Mind

1. W. Somerset Maugham, "The Verger," in *The Complete Short Stories of W. Somerset Maugham,* vol. 3 (Garden City, NY: Doubleday, 1952), pp. 572–578.
2. Anthony Man-Tu Lee and David Weiss, *Zen in 10 Simple Lessons* (Lewes, New Zealand: The Ivy Press Limited, 2002).

Chapter 15: How to Identify Client Needs

1. Francis J. Gouillart and Frederick D. Sturdivant, "Spend a Day in the Life of Your Customer," *Harvard Business Review,* January 1, 1994.

Chapter 17: The Right Foot: Four Ways to Start a Relationship and Position It for the Long Term

1. I have always practiced this in my own advisory work, although the phrase "conceptual agreement" was coined by Alan Weiss, who has authored a number of excellent books on the consulting business (e.g., *The Ultimate Consultant*; New York: Jossey-Bass, 2001).
2. Alan Weiss, *Million Dollar Consulting* (New York: McGraw-Hill Professional Publishing, 1997).

Chapter 18: Five Ways to Grow Your Client Relationships

1. Jagdish Sheth and Andrew Sobel, *Clients for Life: Evolving from an Expert for Hire to an Extraordinary Advisor* (New York: Simon & Schuster, 2000), p. 129.
2. Ford Harding, *Cross-Selling Success* (Avon, MA: Adams Media Corporation, 2002).

Chapter 19: Are Clients Meeting *Your* Expectations?

1. See, for example, Alan Weiss, *Million Dollar Consulting* (New York: McGraw-Hill, 1997).
2. See, for example, David Maister, *True Professionalism* (New York: Free Press, 1997).

Chapter 20: Sustaining and Multiplying

1. Seth Godin, *Permission Marketing* (New York: Simon & Schuster, 1999).
2. Stephen Covey, *The 7 Habits of Highly Effective People* (New York: Simon & Schuster, 1989).
3. Robert Cialdini, *Influence: The Psychology of Persuasion* (New York: William Morrow, 1984), p. 167.

4. See, for example, Bill Gates, *Unlimited Referrals* (Silver Spring, MD: Thunder Hill Press, 1996).

Chapter 21: Merlin: Working a Little Magic with Your Clients

1. For example, see Norma Lorre Goodrich, *Merlin* (New York: Harper-Perennial, 1988).

Chapter 22: 5 Steps to New Business with Old Clients

1. Ianthe Jeanne Dugan, "Depreciated: Did You Hear the One About the Accountant? It's Not Very Funny," *The Wall Street Journal,* March 14, 2002, p. A1.
2. A top Citigroup executive once told me this story: "We had a group of consultants analyze our credit card business, which is an important contributor to corporate profits. They did a very good job during the course of the project, but the final presentation was awkward. After describing their findings, they dedicated the last 45 minutes of the meeting to telling us how important it was for them to help us with implementation. It was embarrassing, and we felt pressured. A slide or two on the subject would have been okay—but they went on and on. Everyone in the audience was uncomfortable. It had the opposite effect to what was intended—it made us want to use them less, not more."

Chapter 23: The Rothschild Bankers: The Power of Unique Capabilities

1. Niall Ferguson, *The House of Rothschild: Money's Prophets 1798–1848* (New York: Penguin Putnam, 1998), p. 88.
2. Ferguson, p. 89.
3. Ferguson, p. 65.
4. Ferguson, p. 77.
5. Ferguson, p. 120.
6. Ferguson, p. 267.
7. Ferguson, p. 105.

Chapter 24: Cultivating the Attitude of Independent Wealth

1. For example, Laurence Hall, "An Honest Look at Our Standards of Truth," *The Star-Ledger Newark,* April 12, 2002, p.23; or Becky Mollenkamp, "When Kids Cheat," *Better Homes and Gardens,* March 2002, p. 82.
2. Mark Albion, *Making a Life, Making a Living* (New York: Warner Books, 2000).

3. Jagdish Sheth and Andrew Sobel, *Clients for Life: Evolving from an Expert for Hire to an Extraordinary Advisor* (New York: Simon & Schuster, 2000), p. 43.

Chapter 25: Managing Client Relationships during Uncertain Times

1. Susan Bishop, "The Strategic Power of Saying No," *Harvard Business Review,* November 11, 1999.
2. Baltasar Gracián, *The Art of Worldly Wisdom* (New York: Doubleday, 1991), p. 152.

Chapter 27: Becoming a Firm That Makes Rain: How Great Organizations Build Clients for Life

1. Daniel Goleman, *Emotional Intelligence* (New York: Bantam, 1997).
2. Interview with Egon Zehnder in "A Simpler Way to Pay," *Harvard Business Review,* April 2001.
3. "Tom Siebel of Siebel Systems: High Tech the Old-Fashioned Way," *Harvard Business Review,* March 2001, p. 118.
4. Ibid., p. 120.

Index

About the Author

Andrew Sobel is a leading authority on client relationships and the skills and strategies required to earn long-term client loyalty. He has spent 22 years as a business advisor to senior executives in over 30 countries around the world, helping leading companies create winning strategies, renew their organizations, and develop client- and customer-focused cultures. His clients range from established public companies such as Citigroup, Cox Communications, and Telecom Italia to a broad variety of professional service firms including Hewitt Associates, Fulbright & Jaworski, and Booz, Allen & Hamilton. He spent 15 years with Gemini Consulting (now Cap Gemini Ernst & Young), cofounding its international practice and serving as a senior vice president and managing director.

Andrew is also coauthor of the acclaimed book, *Clients for Life: Evolving from an Expert for Hire to an Extraordinary Advisor*. His articles and work have appeared in a variety of national magazines and media, including *USA Today, Advertising Age, The HR Executive, Investors Business Daily, Consultants News, Business Law Today,* and *The Dallas Morning News,* and he has been a frequent guest on national network news programs such as ABC's *World News This Morning* and CNN-fn's *For Entrepreneurs Only.*

Andrew speaks frequently to corporate groups and conferences on developing long-term client relationships, and he has worked with many organizations to design and deliver courses and learning programs which teach professionals how to become broad-based, trusted business advisors. His Web site, www.andrewsobel.com, contains a downloadable library of articles on relationship-building as well as several online assessment tools that will enable you to systematically evaluate your and your firm's capacity to build client loyalty. His widely distributed monthly newsletter, *Client Loyalty: Strategies for Building Inner Circle Relationships,* is free and can be subscribed to on his Web site or by sending an e-mail to join-clients@andrewsobel.com.

Andrew graduated cum laude from Middlebury College and earned his MBA from Dartmouth's Tuck School of Business. He is president of his own strategy advisory firm, Andrew Sobel Advisors, Inc. He can be contacted at andrew@andrewsobel.com.